GW00992513

# BEST OF NEW YORK
# FIRST-TIMER TRAVEL GUIDE 2023

"New York Uncovered: The Insider's
Guide to Exploring the City That Never
Sleeps
For First-Time Visitors"

By

SARA KHAN

# TABLE OF CONTENTS

# COPYRIGHT

## ABOUT THE BOOK

Embark on an unforgettable journey through the vibrant streets of the Big Apple with the definitive New York First-Timer Travel Guide 2023. Packed with insider tips, hidden gems, and must-see attractions, this comprehensive guidebook is your ultimate companion for exploring the iconic city that never sleeps.

Whether you're a culture enthusiast, a history buff, a food lover, or an avid adventurer, this meticulously crafted guidebook caters to every traveler's interests and desires. Uncover the magic of New York City as you dive into its rich history, immerse yourself in its diverse neighborhoods, and discover the endless possibilities it has to offer.

Navigate the bustling streets like a true local with detailed maps, transportation guides, and expert advice on the best ways to explore the city. From the iconic landmarks of Times Square, the Statue of Liberty, and Central Park, to the trendy neighborhoods of Brooklyn, SoHo, and Williamsburg, this guide will lead you to the heart and soul of each destination.

Indulge your taste buds in New York's culinary delights, from the world-famous New York-style pizza to the diverse international cuisines found in its many neighborhoods. Unearth the best coffee shops, rooftop bars, and hidden speakeasies that will make your New York experience truly unforgettable.

Beyond the popular tourist spots, this guidebook offers unique and off-the-beaten-path experiences that will provide you with an authentic taste of the city. Explore art galleries in Chelsea, stroll along the High Line, catch a Broadway show, or browse the vintage stores of the Lower East Side.

With practical tips on navigating the city's public transportation system, advice on budget-friendly accommodations, and suggestions for day trips and weekend getaways, this guide ensures that your first visit to New York is smooth, enjoyable, and filled with remarkable memories.

Whether you're planning a short visit or an extended stay, New York First-Timer Travel Guide 2023 is your essential companion to unlock the secrets and wonders of this iconic metropolis. Get ready to be captivated by the energy, diversity, and awe-inspiring beauty of the city that never ceases to amaze.

## WELCOME TO NEW YORK CITY

Welcome to the vibrant and iconic city of New York! Known as the "Big Apple" and the city that never sleeps, New York is a captivating metropolis that offers a truly unforgettable experience. Whether you're a first-time visitor or a returning traveler, prepare to be enchanted by the energy, diversity, and endless possibilities that await you.

As you step foot onto the bustling streets of New York, you'll find yourself immersed in a melting pot of cultures, languages, and cuisines. From the towering skyscrapers that define the iconic Manhattan skyline to the charming brownstones of Brooklyn, each neighborhood has its own distinct character, contributing to the rich tapestry that makes up this magnificent city.

No visit to New York is complete without exploring its world-renowned attractions. Marvel at the architectural masterpiece that is the Statue of Liberty, a symbol of freedom and hope. Take a stroll through the urban oasis of Central Park, where nature thrives amidst the urban jungle. Visit Times Square, where the neon lights illuminate the streets and the city's heartbeat echoes through the crowds.

New York is a global capital of art, culture, and entertainment. Indulge in the vibrant arts scene by visiting the iconic Museum of Modern Art (MoMA) or catching a Broadway show, where you'll witness the magic of live performances. Savor the flavors of the city by dining at diverse culinary establishments, from gourmet Michelin-starred restaurants to beloved food trucks serving mouth watering street food.

Immerse yourself in the city's shopping paradise, with flagship stores and boutiques lining famous streets like Fifth Avenue. From high fashion to independent designers, you'll find a world of fashion at your fingertips.

Catch a game at the hallowed grounds of Yankee Stadium or Madison Square Garden, where you can witness the passion and excitement of New York sports teams.

Above all, it's the people of New York who make this city truly special. New Yorkers are known for their resilience, diversity, and their ability to come together in the face of challenges. Embrace the city's fast-paced rhythm, and you'll find yourself swept up in the collective spirit of ambition and possibility.

So, welcome to New York! Get ready to be captivated by its towering skyscrapers, enchanted by its vibrant neighborhoods, and inspired by its endless opportunities. Whether you're here for business or pleasure, New York promises to leave an indelible mark on your heart and soul. Enjoy your stay and embrace the magic of this extraordinary city!

# CHAPTER 1

# INTRODUCTION TO NEW YORK

Welcome to the vibrant and iconic metropolis of New York City, where dreams are born, and possibilities seem infinite. Known as the "Big Apple," this bustling urban landscape is a melting pot of cultures, ideas, and experiences, pulsating with an energy that is unmatched anywhere else in the world.

Situated in the northeastern United States, New York City is composed of five boroughs—Manhattan, Brooklyn, Queens, The

Bronx, and Staten Island—each with its own distinctive character and allure. From the towering skyscrapers of Manhattan's iconic skyline to the vibrant street art and trendy neighborhoods of Brooklyn, this city is a tapestry of diversity, innovation, and ambition.

New York City has long been regarded as a global center for finance, commerce, media, art, and fashion. Wall Street in Lower Manhattan serves as the heart of the world's financial markets, while Madison Avenue and Fifth Avenue boast renowned shopping districts that attract fashion enthusiasts from around the globe. The city is also a hub for the entertainment industry, with Broadway theaters showcasing the best of live performances, and Hollywood studios producing films and television shows that captivate audiences worldwide.

But New York City is more than just a bustling business hub; it's a cultural powerhouse. The city is home to world-class museums such as the Metropolitan Museum of Art, the Museum of Modern Art (MoMA), and the Guggenheim Museum, where art aficionados can immerse themselves in masterpieces spanning centuries and continents. The city's diverse neighborhoods offer a multitude of culinary delights, ranging from Michelin-starred restaurants to mouthwatering street food carts, showcasing flavors from every corner of the globe.

In addition to its cultural riches, New York City's iconic landmarks are renowned across the globe. The Statue of Liberty, a symbol of freedom and hope, stands tall in the New York Harbor, welcoming visitors from near and far. The Empire State Building, Central Park, Times Square, and the Brooklyn Bridge are just a few of the many architectural marvels that leave visitors in awe of the city's grandeur.

Yet, amidst the hustle and bustle, New York City maintains its sense of community and individuality. Its residents, known as New Yorkers, are known for their resilience, diversity, and spirited nature. The city's neighborhoods, each with its own distinct character, offer a glimpse into the lives of its inhabitants, from the vibrant street life of Chinatown to the bohemian atmosphere of Greenwich Village.

New York City is a place where dreams are pursued and boundaries are pushed. It has inspired countless artists, writers, and innovators, and its spirit continues to captivate those who visit. Whether you're exploring its iconic attractions, savoring its culinary delights, or immersing yourself in its cultural offerings, New York City promises an unforgettable experience that will leave an indelible mark on your heart and soul. Get ready to be swept away by the magic of the "City That Never Sleeps."

## HISTORY, CULTURE AND LANGUAGE

New York City, often referred to as the "Big Apple," is a vibrant and diverse metropolis that stands as a global icon of culture, history, and language. With a rich and complex past, New York City has played a pivotal role in shaping the United States and has become a melting pot of various cultures and languages from around the world. Let's explore the fascinating history, diverse culture, and unique linguistic landscape of this extraordinary city.

## HISTORY:

New York City's history dates back to the early 17th century when it was originally inhabited by various Native American tribes, including the Lenape people. The city's foundation can be traced to the arrival of the Dutch in 1624, who established New Amsterdam as a trading post. In 1664, the British took control of the colony and renamed it New York in honor of the Duke of York.

Throughout its history, New York City has witnessed significant events and transformations. It served as the capital of the United States from 1785 to 1790 and played a vital role in the American Revolution. The city's growth skyrocketed in the 19th and 20th centuries, becoming a major center for immigration, trade, finance, and industry. The construction of iconic landmarks like the Statue of Liberty and the Brooklyn Bridge further solidified its status as a global hub.

**CULTURE:**

New York City's culture is incredibly diverse, drawing influences from various ethnicities and communities that have settled there over the centuries. The city's cultural scene is renowned for its museums, theaters, art galleries, music venues, and culinary delights.

Art and entertainment thrive in New York City, with world-class institutions like the Metropolitan Museum of Art, Museum of Modern Art (MoMA), Broadway theaters, Lincoln Center for the Performing Arts, and the vibrant street art scene in neighborhoods like SoHo and Bushwick.

The city's multiculturalism is evident in its neighborhoods, each with its own distinct character and cultural flavor. From the Italian-American heritage of Little Italy to the vibrant Hispanic culture of East Harlem, from the Jewish heritage of the Lower East Side to the African-American history of Harlem, New York

City offers a rich tapestry of cultures that coexist and interact, creating a unique social fabric.

## LANGUAGE:

New York City is a linguistic mosaic, where numerous languages are spoken due to the diverse immigrant communities and international influence. English is the dominant language and serves as the common means of communication. However, the city is also home to a multitude of other languages, reflecting its cosmopolitan nature.

Spanish is widely spoken throughout the city due to its significant Hispanic population, particularly in neighborhoods like Washington Heights and the Bronx. Other prominent languages include Chinese, Russian, Bengali, Haitian Creole, Korean, Polish, Urdu, and many more. These languages are not only spoken within immigrant communities but have also contributed to the linguistic diversity of the city as a whole.

Additionally, New York City has its own unique linguistic style known as "New York English" or "New Yorkese." It is characterized by distinctive accents, intonation patterns, and a rapid pace of speech. The city's linguistic diversity and the blend of different accents and dialects add to its vibrant tapestry of languages.

In conclusion, New York City's history, culture, and language have intertwined to create a captivating and dynamic urban landscape. Its rich historical legacy, diverse cultural offerings, and multilingualism contribute to its reputation as a global epicenter of art, commerce, and human diversity. New York City stands as a testament to the power of immigration, cultural exchange, and the remarkable human capacity to build a thriving metropolis from humble beginnings.

## GEOGRAPHY OF NEW YORK

New York City, often referred to as NYC, is a vibrant and iconic metropolis located in the northeastern United States. It is situated on the southeastern tip of the state of New York, at the mouth of the Hudson River, where it meets the Atlantic Ocean. The geography of New York

City is diverse and encompasses various landforms, water bodies, and distinct boroughs, making it one of the most geographically fascinating cities in the world.

Manhattan, the heart of the city, is a densely populated island bounded by the Hudson River to the west and the East River to the east. It is known for its iconic skyline, featuring towering skyscrapers such as the Empire State Building and One World Trade Center.

The Bronx is the only borough of New York City located on the mainland, bordered by Westchester County to the north and the Harlem River to the west and south. It is home to diverse neighborhoods, parks, and the renowned Bronx Zoo. Brooklyn, situated on the western end of Long Island, is characterized by its distinct neighborhoods, cultural diversity, and iconic Coney Island beach.

Queens, the largest borough in terms of area, is located on Long Island's eastern end and is surrounded by water bodies such as the East River and the Atlantic Ocean. It is a melting pot of cultures and is known for its residential neighborhoods, diverse communities, and attractions like Flushing Meadows-Corona Park, which hosted the 1964 World's Fair.

Staten Island, often referred to as the "forgotten borough," is located in the southwest part of New York City and is separated from New Jersey by the Arthur Kill and the Kill Van Kull. It is known for its suburban character, open spaces, and the famous Staten Island Ferry, providing breathtaking views of the city skyline.

New York City's geography also includes numerous water bodies that have shaped its history and development. The Hudson River flows along the city's western boundary, offering scenic views and recreational opportunities. The East River, despite its name, is actually a tidal strait that separates Manhattan from Long Island and connects Upper New York Bay with Long Island Sound.

The city's coastal location grants it access to the Atlantic Ocean, with popular beaches like Coney Island and Rockaway Beach drawing crowds during the summer months. The geography of the city's coastline has also influenced its resilience to natural disasters such as hurricanes and storm surges.

In addition to its boroughs and water bodies, New York City is dotted with numerous parks and green spaces. Central Park, located in the heart of Manhattan, is an expansive urban oasis that provides a respite from the bustling city. Other notable parks include Prospect Park in Brooklyn, Flushing Meadows-Corona Park in Queens, and Pelham Bay Park in the Bronx, which is the city's largest park.

Overall, the geography of New York City is a blend of islands, rivers, bays, and diverse neighborhoods. Its unique location, surrounded by water and connected to the Atlantic Ocean, has played a significant role in shaping its history, culture, and iconic skyline. From the bustling streets of Manhattan to the suburban tranquility of Staten Island, the geography of

New York City offers a captivating backdrop to its vibrant urban life.

## GENERAL SURVIVAL TIPS

Surviving in New York City can be an exhilarating experience, but it can also be overwhelming for newcomers and visitors. Here are some general survival tips to help you navigate the bustling streets of the Big Apple:

**Be aware of your surroundings:** New York City is known for its fast-paced environment, so it's important to stay alert and aware of what's happening around you. Pay attention to traffic, pedestrians, and any potential hazards.

**Use public transportation:** NYC has an extensive public transportation system, including buses and subways. Familiarize yourself with the subway lines and bus routes to get around the city efficiently. Use apps or online maps for real-time updates and schedules.

**Avoid rush hours:** Rush hours in NYC can be incredibly crowded, especially during weekdays in the mornings and evenings. If possible, plan your travel outside of these peak times to avoid the crowds and save yourself from unnecessary stress.

**Secure your belongings:** New York City is generally safe, but like any other major city, it's important to take precautions to protect your belongings. Keep your valuables secure and be mindful of your surroundings, especially in crowded areas or on public transportation.

**Stay hydrated and carry snacks:** Exploring the city can be exhausting, so it's essential to stay hydrated. Carry a water bottle with you and consider packing some snacks to keep your energy levels up during your adventures.

**Dress comfortably and wear good walking shoes:** New York City is a walking city, and you'll likely spend a lot of time on your feet. Opt for comfortable clothing and wear shoes that can handle the city's extensive walking paths. Be prepared for varying weather conditions by layering your clothing.

**Research before you go:** Before visiting New York City, do some research about the neighborhoods, attractions, and transportation options. Familiarize yourself with the city's layout and plan your itinerary accordingly. This will help you make the most of your time and navigate the city more efficiently.

**Carry a city map or use a navigation app:** Even though New York City has a well-defined grid system, it's easy to get disoriented, especially in areas with tall buildings that obstruct your view. Carry a city map or use a navigation app on your phone to help you find your way around.

**Stay connected:** Having a working phone and internet connection can be extremely useful in NYC. It allows you to access maps, check transportation updates, and stay connected with friends or emergency services if needed.

**Enjoy the city's diversity:** New York City is a melting pot of cultures, cuisines, and experiences. Embrace the diversity and try to explore different neighborhoods, sample different foods, and engage with the locals. This will enrich your experience and help you appreciate the vibrant spirit of the city.

Remember, surviving in New York City is not just about navigating the streets; it's also about immersing yourself in the unique atmosphere and enjoying everything the city has to offer. So stay safe, be open to new experiences, and make the most of your time in the Big Apple!

# VISITING NEW YORK FOR THE FIRST TIME

Visiting New York for the first time is an exhilarating experience that captivates the senses and immerses you in the vibrant energy of the city that never sleeps. From iconic landmarks to diverse neighborhoods, New York offers a plethora of attractions and activities that will leave you awestruck and longing for more.

Upon arriving in New York, the city's imposing skyline greets you, creating an immediate sense of wonder. The towering skyscrapers, with the Empire State Building and One World Trade Center standing tall, showcase the architectural grandeur and symbolize the city's indomitable spirit. The hustle and bustle of the streets, the honking of yellow taxis, and the sea of people rushing by contribute to the city's constant motion and dynamic atmosphere.

One of the first places you must visit is Times Square. As you step into this bustling hub, you find yourself surrounded by vibrant billboards, flashing lights, and an electrifying energy that seems to pulse through the air. The sheer magnitude of Times Square is awe-inspiring, and it's a place that truly embodies the essence of New York.

From Times Square, you can venture into Central Park, an oasis of green in the midst of the concrete jungle. The park's vast expanse offers a serene respite from the city's chaos. You can take a leisurely stroll along the winding paths, rent a bicycle to explore its hidden corners, or simply relax on one of the park's iconic benches. Central Park provides a refreshing contrast to the urban landscape and allows you to reconnect with nature.

New York is also renowned for its world-class museums and art galleries. The Metropolitan Museum of Art, commonly known as the Met, houses an extensive collection spanning thousands of years and diverse cultures. From ancient Egyptian artifacts to contemporary masterpieces, the Met offers a captivating journey through human history and artistic expression.

For a taste of the city's cultural diversity, a visit to neighborhoods like Chinatown, Little Italy, and Harlem is a must. These vibrant enclaves showcase the multicultural fabric of New York, offering an array of culinary delights, unique shops, and cultural experiences. Exploring the streets of these neighborhoods allows you to witness the blending of traditions and the rich tapestry of cultures that make up the city.

No visit to New York would be complete without taking in the breathtaking views from atop the Empire State Building or the observation deck at One World Trade Center. These iconic landmarks provide a panoramic perspective of the city, allowing you to marvel at the sprawling metropolis stretching out before you.

Additionally, New York's culinary scene is a melting pot of flavors and cuisines. From street food vendors offering hot dogs and pretzels to upscale Michelin-starred restaurants, the city caters to every palate. Don't forget to try a classic New York slice of pizza or indulge in a bagel with cream cheese and lox.

As you navigate the streets of New York, you'll realize that the city's greatest asset is its people. New Yorkers are known for their resilience, diversity, and their unmatched passion for their city. Engage in conversations with locals, listen to their stories, and you'll gain a deeper appreciation for the spirit that drives this vibrant metropolis.

Visiting New York for the first time is an unforgettable adventure that immerses you in a world of sights, sounds, and experiences. From the iconic landmarks to the hidden gems, the city has something to offer every visitor. So, whether you find yourself exploring the grandeur of Manhattan or traversing the charming streets of

Brooklyn, New York will undoubtedly leave an indelible mark on your heart, ensuring that you'll long to return again and again.

# CHAPTER 2

# PLANNING YOUR TRIP TO NEW YORK CITY

Planning a trip to New York City can be an exhilarating experience, as the city offers a vibrant blend of culture, history, and iconic landmarks. To make the most of your visit, careful planning is essential. Here are some key factors to consider when planning your trip to the Big Apple.

Firstly, determine the duration of your stay. New York City has countless attractions, so plan accordingly to ensure you have enough time to explore the highlights. A week-long trip is ideal to experience the city's diverse neighborhoods, museums, and famous sights.

Next, decide on your budget. New York City can be expensive, but there are options to suit every pocket. Research and book accommodation well in advance to secure the best rates. Consider staying in neighborhoods like Midtown or Lower Manhattan for convenience and accessibility to major attractions.

List the sites and activities that are a must-do. The Statue of Liberty, Times Square, Central Park, Empire State Building, and Broadway shows are just a few iconic attractions that should be on your list. Plan your itinerary around these landmarks and allocate enough time for each.

Transportation is crucial in a city as vast as New York. Familiarize yourself with the subway system, which is the most efficient way to get around. Purchase a MetroCard for unlimited rides and plan your routes in advance using online resources or smartphone apps. Taxis and ride-sharing services are also readily available, but they can be more expensive and subject to traffic congestion.

Research the diverse culinary scene in advance, as New York City is a food lover's paradise. From street food to Michelin-starred restaurants, the city offers a vast range of cuisines. Don't miss the chance to try classic New York dishes like bagels, pizza, and hot dogs.

Lastly, be flexible and leave room for unexpected discoveries. New York City is filled with hidden gems and off-the-beaten-path attractions. Embrace the city's energy and immerse yourself in its unique atmosphere.

In conclusion, planning your trip to New York City requires careful consideration of factors such as duration, budget, attractions, transportation, and food. With proper planning, you can make the most of your visit and create unforgettable memories in the city that never sleeps.


## BEST TIME TO VISIT NEW YORK


New York City is a vibrant destination that offers something for everyone throughout the year. The best time to visit depends on your preferences and what you hope to experience in the city. Here are some factors to consider when deciding the ideal time for your trip to New York City:

**Weather:** New York experiences four distinct seasons. Spring (April to June) and fall (September to November) are generally considered the best times to visit due to mild temperatures and pleasant weather. Spring offers

45

blooming flowers and greenery, while fall showcases beautiful foliage. Summers (June to August) can be hot and humid, but it's a great time for outdoor activities. Winters (December to February) can be quite cold, but the city transforms into a winter wonderland with holiday decorations.

**Crowds:** New York City is a popular tourist destination, so expect larger crowds during peak seasons. Summer months and the period between Thanksgiving and New Year's are particularly busy. If you prefer fewer crowds and more affordable accommodations, consider visiting during the shoulder seasons of spring and fall.

**Events and Festivals:** New York City hosts numerous events and festivals throughout the year. Some notable ones include the Macy's

Thanksgiving Day Parade, New Year's Eve in Times Square, St. Patrick's Day Parade, Tribeca Film Festival, and various cultural celebrations. If you have specific events or festivals in mind, plan your visit accordingly.

**Budget:** The cost of accommodation and flights can vary depending on the time of year. High tourist seasons, such as summer and the winter holidays, tend to be more expensive. If you're on a budget, consider visiting during the off-peak seasons for better deals.

**Personal Interests:** New York City offers a diverse range of attractions, from iconic landmarks like the Statue of Liberty and Times Square to world-class museums, Broadway shows, and shopping. Consider your personal interests and activities you'd like to experience.

47

Some attractions may have shorter lines or availability during less busy times.

Ultimately, the best time to visit New York City varies depending on your preferences. Each season has its own unique charm, and the city is bustling year-round. Consider the factors mentioned above, and plan your trip accordingly to make the most of your visit to the Big Apple.

## VISA AND ENTRY REQUIREMENTS

Visa and entry requirements for New York City can vary depending on your country of citizenship. Here is a general overview of the visa and entry requirements for visiting New York City as a tourist:

**Visa Waiver Program (VWP):**

Citizens of certain countries may be eligible to travel to the United States under the Visa Waiver Program. With the help of this program, tourists can stay in the country without a visa for up to 90 days. However, travelers under the VWP must apply for an Electronic System for Travel Authorization (ESTA) before their trip.

**B-1/B-2 Visitor Visa:**

If you are not eligible for the Visa Waiver Program or wish to stay longer than 90 days, you will need to apply for a B-1 (business) or B-2 (tourism) visitor visa at the nearest U.S. embassy or consulate in your home country. This visa allows you to stay in the U.S. for a temporary period.

**Passport Requirements:**

All visitors traveling to New York City must have a valid passport. Your passport should be valid for at least six months beyond your planned departure date from the United States.

**Customs and Border Protection (CBP) Procedures:**

Upon arrival in New York City, you will go through customs and immigration procedures at the port of entry. You will be required to present your passport, visa (if applicable), and any supporting documents, such as your return ticket or proof of accommodation.

**COVID-19 Travel Restrictions:**

Due to the ongoing COVID-19 pandemic, additional travel restrictions and requirements may be in place. It is essential to stay updated with the latest information from the U.S.

Department of State, the Centers for Disease Control and Prevention (CDC), and the U.S. embassy or consulate in your home country.

**Other Entry Requirements:**

While not directly related to visas, it's important to note that travelers to the United States, including New York City, may be subject to additional security measures, such as providing fingerprints and photographs upon arrival.

It is crucial to check the specific requirements and procedures based on your citizenship and individual circumstances. Contacting the nearest U.S. embassy or consulate in your country or visiting the official U.S. government websites can provide the most accurate and up-to-date information regarding visa and entry requirements for New York City.

# PACKING CHECKLIST

Packing for a trip to New York requires careful planning to ensure you have everything you need. Here's a comprehensive packing checklist to help you prepare for your New York travel:

**Clothing:**

Check the weather prediction and prepare by bringing the suitable attire. New York experiences all four seasons, so include items such as T-shirts, sweaters, jeans, shorts, dresses, and a light jacket or coat.

**Comfortable walking shoes:** New York City is known for its walking culture, so pack comfortable shoes to explore the city streets.

**Swimwear:** If you plan to visit during the summer, consider packing swimwear if you want to enjoy the city's beaches or pools.

**Rain gear:** An umbrella or a waterproof jacket can come in handy, especially during the rainy seasons.

**Travel Documents:**

**Valid ID or passport:** Ensure you have a valid ID or passport that will allow you to travel and go through security checkpoints.

Printed or digital copies of travel tickets and hotel reservations.

**New York City map or guidebook:** Although you can use navigation apps, having a physical map or guidebook can be helpful for exploring the city.

**Personal Items:**

**Toiletries:** Toothbrush, toothpaste, shampoo, conditioner, soap, deodorant, and any other personal care items you require.

**Medications:** If you take prescription medications, pack an ample supply for the duration of your trip.

**Glasses or contact lenses:** If you wear them, don't forget to pack your eyewear and any necessary accessories.

**Travel-sized first aid kit:** It's always a good idea to have band-aids, pain relievers, and any other essential medications on hand.

**Electronics and Accessories:**

**Mobile phone and charger:** Keep your phone fully charged and bring a charger or power bank for on-the-go charging.

**Camera:** Capture the memorable moments of your trip with a camera or use your smartphone.

**Adapters and converters:** If you're traveling from a different country, make sure to pack adapters and converters for your electronic devices to fit US outlets.

**Entertainment and Miscellaneous:**

**Books, magazines, or e-readers:** For long flights or downtime, bring reading material to keep yourself entertained.

**Travel-sized games:** Consider packing a deck of cards or portable board games to play with friends or family.

**Snacks and reusable water bottle:** Keep yourself fueled and hydrated during your travels.

**Backpack or day bag:** Carry a lightweight bag to store your essentials while exploring the city.

Remember, this list is a general guideline, and you can modify it according to your personal needs and preferences. Double-check everything before you travel to ensure you haven't forgotten anything essential. Enjoy your trip to New York!

## ESSENTIAL TRAVEL TIPS FOR FIRST-TIMERS

If you're a first-time traveler to New York City, here are some essential travel tips to make your trip smoother and more enjoyable:

**Plan your visit:** Research and plan your itinerary in advance to make the most of your time in NYC. Consider the attractions, landmarks, museums, and neighborhoods you want to explore.

**Choose the right time to visit:** NYC can be crowded throughout the year, so consider visiting during the shoulder seasons (spring or fall) for more pleasant weather and slightly fewer tourists. Winter can be cold, but it offers unique experiences like ice skating in Central Park and the festive holiday atmosphere.

**Pack appropriately:** Check the weather forecast before packing, but always be prepared for unexpected changes in weather. You'll probably be doing a lot of walking, so you need to wear comfortable walking shoes.

**Use public transportation:** NYC has an extensive public transportation system, including the subway and buses. It's the most efficient way to get around the city, avoiding traffic and parking hassles. Purchase a MetroCard for easy access.

**Be cautious with your belongings:** New York City is generally safe, but it's always advisable to keep an eye on your belongings. Be cautious in crowded areas and avoid displaying expensive items.

**Explore different neighborhoods:** NYC is made up of diverse neighborhoods, each with its own character and attractions. Take the time to explore areas like Times Square, Central Park, Brooklyn, SoHo, Greenwich Village, and others.

**Try local food:** New York City is famous for its diverse culinary scene. Don't miss the chance to try classic foods like bagels, pizza, hot dogs, pastrami sandwiches, and ethnic cuisines from around the world.

**Purchase a CityPASS or Explorer Pass:** If you plan to visit multiple attractions, consider buying a CityPASS or Explorer Pass. These passes offer discounted access to popular sites and can save you money.

**Take in the views:** Enjoy panoramic views of the city by visiting observation decks like the Empire State Building, Top of the Rock, or the One World Observatory. You can also take a free ride on the Staten Island Ferry for views of the Statue of Liberty.

**Embrace the local culture:** New Yorkers are known for their fast-paced lifestyle, but they're also helpful and friendly. Engage with locals, experience the city's vibrant art scene, catch a Broadway show, or attend live performances.

**Be mindful of your budget:** New York City can be expensive, so plan your budget accordingly. Look for free or low-cost activities, explore affordable dining options, and consider using discount websites for deals on attractions.

**Have a map or navigation app:** NYC can be overwhelming with its grid system, so having a map or a reliable navigation app on your phone will help you navigate the city streets with ease.

Remember, New York City is a dynamic and exciting destination. Embrace the energy, take your time to explore, and soak up the vibrant atmosphere. Enjoy your trip!

## TRAVEL BUDGET ESTIMATION

Estimating a travel budget for New York City can vary depending on your travel preferences, accommodation choices, dining options, and activities you plan to engage in. However, I can provide you with a general overview of the average costs associated with visiting New York City. Keep in mind that prices can fluctuate over time, so it's essential to research up-to-date information for accurate budget planning. Here are some major expense categories to consider:

**Accommodation:**

**Budget hotels/Hostels:** $100-$200 per night
**Mid-range hotels:** $200-$400 per night
**Luxury hotels:** $400+ per night
**Transportation:**

**Taxi/Uber:** Starting at $2.50 plus additional charges per mile or minute

**Subway/Bus fare:** $2.75 per ride (metro card discounts available for multiple rides)

**Rental car (if applicable):** $50-$150 per day, excluding parking fees.

**Food:**

**Inexpensive meals (street food, fast food):** $10-$15 per meal

**Mid-range restaurants:** $20-$40 per meal

**High-end restaurants:** $50+ per meal.

**Attractions and Activities:**

**Museum admission fees:** $20-$30 per person

**Broadway shows:** $50-$250+ per ticket

**Sightseeing tours:** $30-$100+ per person.

**Miscellaneous:**

**Shopping:** Varied depending on your preferences

**Tips and gratuities:** 15-20% of the bill at restaurants and for services

**Souvenirs and other personal expenses:** Varied depending on your preferences

It's important to note that prices can vary significantly depending on the season, special events, and demand.

Additionally, attractions like Times Square, Central Park, and walking across the Brooklyn Bridge are free and can be enjoyed without any cost.

To get a more accurate estimate, consider creating a detailed itinerary with specific activities and their associated costs.

# CHAPTER 3

# TRANSPORTATION OPTIONS TO NEW YORK

There are several transportation options available to travel to New York City. Here are some popular choices:

**Air Travel:** If you are traveling from a long distance or another country, flying to one of New York City's airports is a convenient option. The city has three major airports: Newark Liberty International Airport (EWR), John F. Kennedy International Airport (JFK), and LaGuardia Airport (LGA). All three airports are well-connected and offer numerous domestic and international flights.

**Train:** Amtrak is a popular train service in the United States, and it provides connections to various cities, including New York City. If you are traveling from nearby regions or cities like Boston, Philadelphia, or Washington D.C., taking a train to New York City can be a convenient and scenic option. Penn Station is the main railway station in New York City.

**Bus:** There are several bus companies that operate routes to New York City from various locations. Companies like Greyhound, Megabus, and BoltBus offer affordable and convenient bus services. The city has several bus terminals, including the Port Authority Bus Terminal in Midtown Manhattan.

**Car:** If you prefer driving, you can reach New York City by car. However, keep in mind that traffic in the city can be heavy, and parking can be expensive and limited. It is advisable to research parking options and consider using public transportation once you arrive in the city.

**Subway:** Once you are in New York City, the subway system is an efficient way to get around. It covers a vast network of routes and connects to various neighborhoods and attractions. The subway operates 24/7, but it can be crowded during peak hours.

**Taxis and Rideshares:** Taxis are readily available in New York City, and you can easily hail one from the street. Rideshare services like Uber and Lyft are also popular and offer convenient transportation options. These services are accessible through smartphone apps.

**Ferries:** New York City is surrounded by water, and there are several ferry services available. They offer scenic views and connect Manhattan to destinations like Staten Island, Brooklyn, and New Jersey. The Staten Island Ferry is a popular option for tourists as it provides excellent views of the Statue of Liberty and the Manhattan skyline.

It is essential to consider factors like cost, travel distance, and convenience when choosing the transportation option that best suits your needs.

## BEST WAYS TO REACH NEW YORK

There are several ways to reach New York depending on your location and preferences. Here are some of the best ways to reach New York:

**By Air:** Flying to one of New York City's major airports is a popular choice for domestic and international travelers. John F. Kennedy International Airport (JFK), LaGuardia Airport (LGA), and Newark Liberty International Airport (EWR) are the primary airports serving the area. Numerous airlines operate regular flights to these airports, making air travel a convenient option.

**By Train:** Amtrak, the national rail service, offers train services to New York City. If you are coming from nearby cities such as Boston, Philadelphia, or Washington D.C., taking a train can be a comfortable and scenic way to reach New York. The iconic Penn Station is the main rail hub in the city.

**By Bus:** Several bus companies provide transportation services to New York City from various locations. Companies like Greyhound, Megabus, and BoltBus offer affordable fares and frequent schedules, making bus travel a popular choice for budget-conscious travelers.

**By Car:** If you prefer driving or have more flexibility in your schedule, you can reach New York City by car. However, keep in mind that driving in the city can be challenging due to traffic congestion and limited parking options. It's advisable to research parking options in advance or consider using park-and-ride facilities located outside the city.

**By Ferry:** If you are traveling from nearby locations such as New Jersey or Staten Island, you can reach New York City by ferry. The

Staten Island Ferry, for example, offers free service between Staten Island and Manhattan, providing scenic views of the Statue of Liberty and the city skyline.

Once you arrive in New York, you can utilize the city's extensive public transportation system, including the subway, buses, taxis, and ride-sharing services, to navigate around the city and reach your desired destination.

## FLIGHT OPTIONS AND AIRLINES

John F. Kennedy International Airport (JFK), LaGuardia Airport (LGA), and Newark Liberty International Airport (EWR) are just a few of the airports that serve New York City. These airports are served by a variety of airlines and provide a wide range of flying options. Some of the main airlines with operations in New York City are listed below:

**Delta Air Lines:** Delta is one of the largest airlines in the United States and operates a significant number of flights from all three major airports in New York City.

**American Airlines:** American Airlines is another major carrier that offers a wide range of domestic and international flights from New York City.

**United Airlines:** United Airlines operates flights from all three airports in the New York City area and provides both domestic and international service.

**JetBlue Airways:** JetBlue is a low-cost carrier based in New York City and has a strong presence at JFK and LaGuardia airports.

**Southwest Airlines:** Southwest is a popular low-cost airline in the United States and operates flights primarily from LaGuardia and Newark airports.

**Spirit Airlines:** Spirit is another low-cost carrier that serves New York City, primarily operating from LaGuardia and Newark airports.

**British Airways:** British Airways offers flights between New York City and London, and it operates from JFK airport.

**Virgin Atlantic:** Virgin Atlantic is another airline that provides flights between New York City and London, with operations at JFK airport.

**Air France:** Air France operates flights between New York City and Paris and serves both JFK and Newark airports.

**Lufthansa:** Lufthansa offers flights between New York City and Frankfurt, and it operates from JFK airport.

These are just a few examples of the many airlines serving New York City. Depending on your specific travel needs and destinations, you may find other airlines operating at these airports as well. It's always a good idea to check with the airports' websites or use flight search engines to explore the available flight options.

## LAND TRANSPORTATION OPTIONS

In New York City, there are several land transportation options available for getting around the city. Here are some of the common modes of transportation:

**Subway:** The New York City Subway is a vast and extensive network of underground trains that cover the five boroughs of the city. It is one of the most popular and efficient ways to travel within NYC. The subway operates 24 hours a day, seven days a week, and has multiple lines that connect various neighborhoods and landmarks.

**Bus:** The Metropolitan Transportation Authority (MTA) operates an extensive bus network throughout New York City. Buses are a convenient mode of transportation, especially for reaching areas not served by the subway. Like the subway, buses operate 24/7, and you can use your MetroCard to pay the fare.

**Taxis:** Yellow taxis are a common sight on the streets of New York City. You can hail a taxi by raising your hand or find them at designated taxi stands. Taxis operate 24/7 and can be a convenient option for shorter trips or when you have heavy luggage.

**Ride-Sharing Services:** App-based ride-sharing services like Uber, Lyft, and Via are widely available in New York City. You can use their mobile apps to request a ride, and a driver will pick you up at your location. Ride-sharing services offer the convenience of door-to-door transportation and are an alternative to traditional taxis.

**Bicycles:** Citi Bike is a popular bike-sharing program in New York City. You can rent a bike from one of the many Citi Bike stations located throughout the city and return it to any other station when you're done. Bicycles are a great option for short trips, and New York City has been working to expand its bike lanes and make the city more bike-friendly.

**Walking:** New York City is a highly walkable city, especially in areas with high pedestrian traffic. Walking can be a pleasant way to explore the city, particularly in areas like Manhattan where many attractions are within walking distance of each other.

It's worth noting that New York City experiences heavy traffic congestion, especially during peak hours. Depending on your destination and the time of day, certain transportation options may be more efficient than others. It's advisable to check transit schedules, consider traffic conditions, and plan your route accordingly.

## TRAVELING BY CRUISE SHIP

Traveling by cruise ship to New York City can be a fantastic and unique experience. While I can provide you with some general information, please keep in mind that specific details may vary depending on the cruise line, departure port, and itinerary. Here are some key points to consider:

**Cruise Lines:** Several major cruise lines offer itineraries that include New York City as a port of call or embarkation/disembarkation point. Some popular cruise lines that operate in this region include Norwegian Cruise Line, Royal Caribbean International, Carnival Cruise Line, and Cunard Line.

**Ports:** Most cruises to New York City dock at the Manhattan Cruise Terminal, located on the west side of Manhattan. This terminal provides easy access to many of the city's iconic attractions, such as Times Square, Central Park, and the Statue of Liberty.

**Itineraries:** Cruises to New York City can range from short trips along the Eastern Seaboard to transatlantic voyages originating from European ports. The duration of your cruise will depend on the specific itinerary you choose.

**Attractions:** New York City offers a wealth of world-famous attractions that you can explore during your visit. Some popular landmarks include the Statue of Liberty, Times Square, Central Park, the Empire State Building, the Metropolitan Museum of Art, and Broadway theaters. Additionally, you can enjoy diverse culinary experiences, shopping, and cultural events.

**Pre- and Post-Cruise Stay:** If you have time before or after your cruise, consider spending a few days in New York City to fully experience the city. You can book a hotel and explore the city's attractions at your leisure.

**Transportation:** The Manhattan Cruise Terminal is easily accessible by various means of transportation. You can take a taxi, use rideshare services like Uber or Lyft, or utilize public transportation options such as the subway or buses. The availability of parking facilities for personal vehicles may vary, so it's best to check with the cruise line or terminal authorities in advance.

**Immigration and Customs:** If you are arriving in New York City from an international location, you will need to go through immigration and customs procedures at the cruise terminal. Ensure that you have all appropriate travel documentation, such as a current passport and any applicable visas.

**Weather and Season:** New York City experiences four distinct seasons, so the weather conditions can vary depending on the time of year. Summers are generally warm and humid, while winters can be cold with occasional snowfall. It's advisable to check the weather forecast for your travel dates and pack accordingly.

Remember to consult with your chosen cruise line or a travel agent for the most accurate and up-to-date information regarding cruise itineraries, schedules, and any specific requirements or restrictions. Enjoy your cruise to New York City.

# BUDGET-FRIENDLY TIPS FOR TRANSPORTATION

New York City can be an expensive place to navigate, but there are several budget-friendly transportation options available. Here are some tips to help you get around NYC without breaking the bank:

**Walking:** New York City is a highly walkable city, especially in Manhattan. Many of the popular attractions and neighborhoods are within a reasonable walking distance.

**Public transportation:** The Metropolitan Transportation Authority (MTA) operates an extensive network of subways and buses throughout the city. The subway is the most cost-effective way to get around. Consider getting a MetroCard, which offers discounted fares compared to paying in cash. You can purchase an unlimited weekly or monthly MetroCard if you plan to use the subway frequently.

**Biking:** Citi Bike is a bike-sharing program available in New York City. It offers an affordable way to explore the city on two wheels. You can rent a bike for a short duration and return it to any of the numerous docking stations across the city.

**Staten Island Ferry:** If you want to enjoy a scenic view of the Statue of Liberty and the Manhattan skyline, take a ride on the Staten Island Ferry. It's a free ferry service that operates between Manhattan and Staten Island, offering beautiful views without spending a dime.

**Ride-sharing services:** Services like Uber and Lyft are convenient for getting around the city. While they may not always be the cheapest option, they can be affordable if you're sharing the ride with others. Look out for any ongoing promotions or discounts offered by these companies.

**Off-peak travel:** If you can, try to avoid peak travel times when using public transportation. Fares may be slightly lower during non-rush hours, and you'll have a better chance of finding a seat on the subway or bus.

**Group transportation:** If you're traveling with a group, consider using group transportation options like vans or minibosses. These can be more cost-effective compared to individual fares on public transportation, especially when splitting the cost among several people.

**Plan your trips efficiently:** Before heading out, plan your route to optimize your travel and minimize unnecessary transfers or backtracking. This will help you save both time and money.

Remember to check for any service changes, delays, or disruptions on the MTA website or through their official app. Being aware of any updates can help you plan your transportation accordingly.

# CHAPTER 4

# ACCOMMODATION OPTIONS IN NEW YORK

New York City offers a wide range of accommodation options to suit various budgets and preferences. Here are some popular choices:

88

**Hotels:** NYC has numerous hotels ranging from budget-friendly options to luxury establishments. You can find internationally renowned chains, boutique hotels, and iconic landmarks like The Plaza. Prices vary depending on the location and amenities.

**Hostels:** For budget travelers or those looking to meet fellow travelers, hostels are a good option. You'll find dormitory-style accommodations with shared facilities, as well as private rooms in some hostels.

**Vacation Rentals:** Websites like Airbnb offer a variety of vacation rentals, including apartments, lofts, and townhouses. These can be a good choice for those seeking a home-like experience and more space. However, make sure to check the local regulations regarding short-term rentals.

**Bed and Breakfasts:** There are charming bed and breakfast establishments throughout the city, especially in neighborhoods like Brooklyn and Harlem. These offer a cozy atmosphere and a personal touch.

**Extended Stay Hotels:** If you're planning a longer stay, extended stay hotels provide apartment-style accommodations with kitchenettes or full kitchens. They are suitable for both business travelers and tourists.

**Serviced Apartments:** NYC also has serviced apartments that combine the comforts of home with hotel-like amenities. They are fully furnished and offer services such as housekeeping and concierge.

**Boutique Hotels:** Boutique hotels provide unique and stylish accommodations with personalized service. They often have a distinct theme or design aesthetic, making for a memorable stay.

When choosing your accommodation, consider factors like location, budget, amenities, and the purpose of your visit. It's also advisable to book in advance, especially during peak travel seasons, to secure the best options.

## HOTELS AND RESORTS

Here are some popular hotels and resorts in New York City along with their estimated price ranges. Please note that prices can vary depending on factors such as the season, availability, and room type.

**The Plaza Hotel:** One of the most iconic hotels in NYC, known for its luxury and historic charm. Prices start at around $700 per night.

**The St. Regis New York:** A prestigious hotel offering elegance and top-notch service. Prices start at approximately $800 per night.

**The Mandarin Oriental, New York:** Located in Columbus Circle with stunning views of Central Park and the Manhattan skyline. Prices start at around $800 per night.

**The Ritz-Carlton New York, Central Park:** A luxurious hotel overlooking Central Park, offering upscale amenities. Prices start at approximately $600 per night.

**The Waldorf Astoria New York:** A landmark hotel with a rich history and elegant accommodations. Prices start at around $500 per night.

**The Peninsula New York:** A five-star hotel known for its impeccable service and luxurious rooms. Prices start at approximately $600 per night.

**The Four Seasons Hotel New York:** Located in Midtown Manhattan, offering lavish rooms and exceptional service. Prices start at around $800 per night.

**The Lotte New York Palace:** A grand hotel featuring spacious rooms and a prime location near Rockefeller Center. Prices start at approximately $400 per night.

**The Standard High Line:** A trendy hotel in the Meatpacking District, known for its stylish design and vibrant atmosphere. Prices start at around $300 per night.

**The Ace Hotel New York:** A boutique hotel in Midtown Manhattan, offering a hip and eclectic vibe. Prices start at approximately $200 per night.

Please keep in mind that these prices are approximate and subject to change. It's always a good idea to check with the specific hotel for the most up-to-date pricing and availability.

## VACATION RENTALS AND APARTMENTS

New York City is a popular destination for tourists and travelers, offering a wide range of vacation rentals and apartments to suit different budgets and preferences. Whether you're looking for a short-term stay or a longer vacation, there are various options available. Here are some key points to consider:

**Vacation Rental Platforms:** Websites such as Airbnb, Vrbo (formerly HomeAway), Booking.com, and TripAdvisor offer numerous vacation rentals and apartments in New York City. These platforms allow you to browse through a variety of properties, compare prices, read reviews, and book directly with the property owners or management companies.

**Neighborhoods:** New York City is made up of five boroughs—Manhattan, Brooklyn, Queens, The Bronx, and Staten Island—and each borough has its own distinct neighborhoods. The choice of neighborhood depends on your preferences, budget, and proximity to attractions or areas of interest. Manhattan is the most popular borough for tourists, with neighborhoods like Midtown, Lower Manhattan, and the Upper West Side being popular choices.

**Rental Types:** Vacation rentals in New York City can range from single rooms or studio apartments to entire houses or luxury penthouses. Consider the size of your group, desired amenities, and the length of your stay when selecting a rental. Apartments with kitchens can be a good option if you prefer cooking your own meals.

**Pricing:** Vacation rental prices in New York City vary greatly depending on factors such as location, size, amenities, and seasonal demand. Manhattan tends to be more expensive than other boroughs. It's important to set a budget and search within your price range. Keep in mind that additional charges like cleaning fees and security deposits may apply.

**Safety and Regulations:** When booking vacation rentals, it's essential to prioritize safety and legality. Ensure that the property you choose complies with local regulations and is listed on reputable platforms. Read reviews from previous guests to get a sense of the property's quality and the host's reliability.

**Booking in Advance:** New York City is a popular destination year-round, so it's advisable to book your vacation rental well in advance, especially if you plan to visit during peak seasons or holidays. This will increase your chances of finding the ideal property and potentially secure better prices.

**Alternative Options:** In addition to vacation rentals, New York City also offers various other accommodation options, including hotels, hostels, and extended-stay residences. Depending on your needs and preferences, you may explore these alternatives as well.

Remember to thoroughly research your chosen rental, communicate with the host or property owner, and review the terms and conditions before finalizing your booking. This will help ensure a smooth and enjoyable experience during your stay in New York City.

## CAMPING IN NEW YORK

Camping in New York can be a wonderful experience, offering a chance to connect with nature and explore the state's beautiful outdoor areas. Whether you're interested in pitching a tent, setting up an RV, or renting a cabin, New York has a variety of camping options to suit different preferences. Here are some key points to consider when planning a camping trip in New York:

**State Parks:** New York is home to numerous state parks that provide camping facilities. Some popular options include Letchworth State Park, Allegany State Park, Watkins Glen State Park, and Harriman State Park. These parks offer a range of amenities, such as designated camping areas, picnic tables, restrooms, and fire pits.

**Adirondack Park:** The Adirondack Park, located in northern New York, is a vast wilderness area known for its pristine lakes, mountains, and forests. It offers a wide range of camping opportunities, from backcountry camping to developed campgrounds. The High Peaks region is particularly popular among hikers and outdoor enthusiasts.

**Catskill Mountains:** The Catskill Mountains, located north of New York City, are another popular destination for camping. The Catskills offer a variety of campgrounds, including those near rivers, lakes, and hiking trails. The region is known for its scenic beauty, waterfalls, and opportunities for outdoor activities like fishing, hiking, and birdwatching.

**Fire Island National Seashore:** If you're interested in camping by the beach, Fire Island National Seashore is a great option. Located off the southern coast of Long Island, it offers several campgrounds where you can enjoy sandy beaches, dunes, and beautiful sunsets. However, note that some campgrounds may require advance reservations.

**Camping Regulations:** When camping in New York, it's important to be aware of the regulations and guidelines set by the specific park or campground you plan to visit. These may include rules regarding campfire safety, waste disposal, pet policies, and quiet hours. Make sure to check the official websites or contact the park authorities for up-to-date information.

**Reservation and Permits:** Many campgrounds in New York require advance reservations, especially during peak seasons. It's advisable to check availability and make reservations well in advance to secure your preferred camping spot. Additionally, certain areas, such as the backcountry in the Adirondacks, may require permits for camping, so be sure to research and obtain any necessary permits before your trip.

**Weather and Seasonal Considerations:** New York experiences distinct seasons, so it's important to consider the weather conditions when planning your camping trip. Spring and fall offer milder temperatures and colorful foliage, while summers can be warm and humid. Winters are typically cold, with the possibility of heavy snowfall in some areas. Pack appropriate clothing and gear based on the season and expected weather conditions.

Remember to practice Leave No Trace principles, respect the environment, and follow all camping regulations to help preserve the natural beauty of New York's outdoor spaces.

Enjoy your camping adventure in the Empire State.

## HOSTELS AND BUDGET ACCOMMODATIONS

New York City is known for being an expensive destination, but there are still several options for budget accommodations, including hostels. Here are some popular hostels and budget accommodations in New York City:

**HI NYC Hostel:** Located on the Upper West Side, this hostel is one of the largest in North America. It offers affordable dormitory-style rooms, private rooms, and numerous amenities such as a communal kitchen, free Wi-Fi, and organized activities for guests.

**The Local NYC:** Situated in Long Island City, Queens, this hostel provides a more relaxed and artistic atmosphere. It offers private rooms and dormitories, along with amenities like a bar, a communal kitchen, free Wi-Fi, and a common area with games and events.

**Chelsea International Hostel:** This hostel is centrally located in Chelsea and offers both private and shared rooms. It has a communal kitchen, free Wi-Fi, a TV lounge, and laundry facilities.

**Jazz on Columbus Circle Hostel:** Located near Central Park, this hostel offers affordable dormitory-style rooms and private rooms. It features a fully equipped kitchen, a common area with a pool table, a jazz club, and free Wi-Fi.

**Pod 51 Hotel:** While not a traditional hostel, Pod 51 Hotel in Midtown Manhattan offers compact and affordable rooms with shared bathrooms. It has a communal lounge, a rooftop deck, a cafe, and a 24-hour fitness center.

**Broadway Hotel and Hostel:** Situated on the Upper West Side, this budget accommodation offers private rooms and dormitories. It provides a shared kitchen, a common room with a pool table, free Wi-Fi, and a rooftop terrace.

**Q4 Hotel and Hostel:** Located in Queens, this hostel offers both private rooms and dormitories. It features a communal kitchen, a lounge area, free Wi-Fi, and an outdoor courtyard.

Remember to book in advance, especially during peak tourist seasons, to secure the best rates and availability. Additionally, always read reviews and check the hotel's website for specific information about amenities, policies, and any additional charges.

## CHAPTER 5

## NAVIGATING THE CITY: TRANSPORTATION GUIDE

Navigating New York City can be exciting and sometimes overwhelming due to its size and bustling streets. However, there are several transportation options available to help you get around the city efficiently. Here's a transportation guide to help you navigate New York City:

**Subway:** The subway system is one of the most popular and convenient ways to travel around NYC. It operates 24/7 and covers all five boroughs. You can purchase a MetroCard at any subway station to pay for your rides. Be sure to check the subway map for the route you need to take.

**Buses:** The bus network in New York City is extensive and covers areas not served by the subway. Buses operate 24/7, and you can also use the MetroCard to pay for your bus fare. Bus stops are marked with signs indicating the routes that stop there. You can use the MTA Bus Time app or website to track bus locations and estimated arrival times.

**Taxis:** Yellow taxis are a common sight in New York City. You can hail a taxi from the street or find them at designated taxi stands. Taxis charge by the meter, and it's customary to tip the driver around 15-20% of the fare.

**Ride-Sharing Services:** Services like Uber and Lyft are widely available in NYC. You can book a ride through their respective apps. They offer convenient door-to-door transportation options, and you can often choose between different vehicle types depending on your needs.

**Bicycles:** Citi Bike is a popular bike-sharing program in NYC. You can rent a bike from any of the docking stations located throughout the city. There are also bike lanes in many areas, making cycling a viable transportation option.

**Walking:** New York City is a pedestrian-friendly city, and walking is a great way to explore certain neighborhoods. Many attractions, such as Central Park, Times Square, and the High Line, are easily accessible on foot. Just remember to obey traffic signals and be aware of your surroundings.

**Ferries:** NYC has several ferry services that can take you across the city's waterways. The Staten Island Ferry is a free option that offers fantastic views of the Statue of Liberty and the Manhattan skyline. There are also other ferry routes available, including the NYC Ferry, which connects various parts of the city.

It's worth noting that traffic congestion can be heavy in certain areas of NYC, so public transportation or walking may be faster options during peak hours. Additionally, consider using navigation apps like Google Maps or Citymapper to help you plan your routes and estimate travel times accurately.

Lastly, keep in mind that New York City is an ever-changing environment, so it's a good idea to stay updated on any changes or service disruptions by checking the Metropolitan Transportation Authority (MTA) website or following their social media accounts.

## PUBLIC TRANSPORTATION

Public transportation in New York City is an integral part of the city's transportation system. It is known for its extensive network, which includes subways, buses, and commuter trains. Here's an overview of the public transportation options available in New York City:

**Subway:** The New York City Subway is one of the largest and oldest rapid transit systems in the world. It consists of 27 subway lines and serves the five boroughs of New York City. The subway operates 24 hours a day, seven days a week, and is a popular mode of transportation for both residents and visitors.

**Buses:** The Metropolitan Transportation Authority (MTA) operates a vast bus network that covers all five boroughs of New York City. Buses run throughout the day and night, providing extensive coverage in areas not served by the subway. The routes and schedules are well-coordinated with the subway system.

**Commuter Trains:** The MTA also operates commuter trains that connect New York City with the surrounding suburbs. The two primary commuter rail services are Metro-North Railroad, serving areas north and east of the city, and the Long Island Rail Road (LIRR), serving Long Island and parts of Queens.

**Ferries:** The NYC Ferry service offers a scenic and efficient way to travel across the city's waterways. It connects various neighborhoods in Manhattan, Brooklyn, Queens, and the Bronx. The ferries provide an alternative transportation option for both commuters and tourists.

**Access-A-Ride:** Access-A-Ride is a shared-ride, paratransit service for individuals with disabilities who are unable to use public buses or subways. It provides door-to-door transportation within the five boroughs.

**Bike Sharing:** New York City has a bike-sharing program called Citi Bike, which allows residents and visitors to rent bicycles for short trips. The program has numerous docking stations throughout the city, making it convenient to pick up and drop off bikes.

It's important to note that fares are required for most forms of public transportation in New York City. The MTA offers various fare payment options, including MetroCards and contactless payment methods like Apple Pay and Google Pay.

It's also worth mentioning that the MTA provides real-time service updates, maps, and trip planners through its website and mobile apps, which can be useful for navigating the public transportation system in New York City.

## TAXIS AND RIDESHARES

Taxis and rideshares are common modes of transportation in New York City. They provide convenient options for residents and visitors to navigate the city's busy streets. Here's some information about taxis and rideshares in New York City:

**Taxis (Yellow Cabs):** Yellow taxis are iconic in New York City and can be hailed from the street or found at designated taxi stands throughout the city. These taxis are operated by licensed drivers who undergo extensive training and testing. Taxis charge fares based on a meter that calculates distance and time traveled. They accept cash, credit cards, and some also offer mobile payment options.

**Rideshares (Uber, Lyft, etc.):** Rideshare services like Uber and Lyft are popular alternatives to traditional taxis in New York City. Users can request a ride using a mobile app, and a nearby driver will pick them up in their personal vehicle. Rideshares provide a convenient and often cheaper option for transportation. Payment is typically made through the app using a registered credit card.

**Accessibility:** Both taxis and rideshares in New York City offer accessible options for passengers with disabilities. Taxis are required to have wheelchair-accessible vehicles in their fleets, while rideshares also offer wheelchair-accessible options upon request. Additionally, rideshares have options for passengers with specific accessibility needs, such as extra space or assistance.

**Regulations:** Taxis in New York City are heavily regulated by the New York City Taxi and Limousine Commission (TLC). The TLC sets requirements for vehicle standards, driver qualifications, and fare regulations. Rideshare services are also regulated by the TLC, which includes driver background checks, vehicle inspections, and insurance requirements.

**Pricing:** Taxis in New York City have a standard fare structure, which includes a base fare, additional charges for distance traveled, and waiting time. Rideshares, on the other hand, use dynamic pricing based on supply and demand. During periods of high demand, prices may increase significantly. The app usually provides an upfront estimate of the fare before confirming the ride.

**Availability:** Taxis are widely available throughout New York City, particularly in busy areas like Manhattan. Rideshares also have a strong presence and can often be found within minutes, even in less densely populated areas. Both taxis and rideshares operate 24/7, providing transportation options at any time of the day or night.

It's important to note that specific details, regulations, and pricing may vary over time. It's recommended to refer to official websites and apps of taxi and rideshare services in New York City for the most up-to-date information and to ensure a safe and reliable transportation experience.

## BIKING AND WALKING

Biking and walking are popular modes of transportation in New York City, offering residents and visitors an efficient and enjoyable way to get around. The city has made significant efforts to improve cycling infrastructure and promote pedestrian-friendly streets, making it increasingly bike and pedestrian-friendly.

**Biking in New York City:**

**Bike Lanes:** The city has implemented an extensive network of bike lanes throughout the five boroughs, providing designated areas for cyclists to ride safely. These lanes are typically marked with signage or separated from vehicle traffic by physical barriers.

**Citi Bike:** Citi Bike is a bike-sharing program available in Manhattan, Brooklyn, Queens, and parts of the Bronx. Users can rent bicycles from docking stations located throughout the city and return them to any other docking station within the system.

**Bike Paths and Greenways:** New York City offers a variety of dedicated bike paths and greenways, providing scenic routes for cyclists.

Examples include the Hudson River Greenway, the Manhattan Waterfront Greenway, and the Brooklyn Waterfront Greenway.

**Bike-Friendly Policies:** The city has implemented policies to support biking, such as allowing cyclists to bring their bikes on select subway and train lines outside of peak hours. Many buses also have bike racks installed.

**Walking in New York City:**

**Pedestrian-Friendly Streets:** New York City has been actively working to create more pedestrian-friendly streets, with initiatives like the "Open Streets" program that temporarily closes selected streets to vehicles, allowing pedestrians to walk freely.

**Sidewalks:** Sidewalks are ubiquitous throughout the city, providing safe walking spaces for pedestrians. However, they can get crowded, especially in densely populated areas and during peak hours.

**Pedestrian Plazas:** The city has transformed several public spaces into pedestrian plazas, such as Times Square and Herald Square. These areas offer seating, pedestrian-only zones, and improved walking conditions.

**Parks and Green Spaces:** New York City boasts numerous parks and green spaces where people can walk, jog, or simply enjoy the outdoors. Famous examples include Central Park, Prospect Park, and the High Line.

**Safety Considerations:**

When biking or walking in New York City, it's important to prioritize safety.

**Obey Traffic Laws:** Cyclists should follow the same traffic rules as vehicles, including stopping at red lights and yielding to pedestrians. Pedestrians should use crosswalks and wait for traffic signals.

**Use Bike Helmets:** If you choose to bike, wearing a helmet is strongly recommended to protect yourself in case of accidents.

**Be Alert:** Stay aware of your surroundings, especially when crossing streets or biking alongside traffic. Keep an eye out for pedestrians, vehicles, and other cyclists.

**Lock Bicycles Securely:** If you own a bike, invest in a sturdy lock and secure it properly when leaving it unattended to prevent theft.

By leveraging biking and walking in New York City, you can experience the city's vibrant neighborhoods, explore its iconic landmarks, and enjoy a more active and environmentally friendly way of getting around.

# CHAPTER 6

# TOP ATTRACTIONS AND LANDMARKS

New York City is home to numerous iconic attractions and landmarks that draw millions of visitors each year. Here are some of the top attractions and landmarks you should consider exploring in the city:

**Statue of Liberty:** Located on Liberty Island, the Statue of Liberty is an enduring symbol of freedom and a must-visit landmark. Take a ferry ride to the island and climb to the crown for stunning views of the city.

**Times Square:** Known as "The Crossroads of the World," Times Square is a bustling hub of activity, with its bright neon billboards, theaters, shops, and restaurants. It's particularly famous for its New Year's Eve ball drop.

**Central Park:** This expansive urban park in the heart of Manhattan offers a tranquil escape from the city's hustle and bustle. Explore the park's walking trails, lakes, meadows, and iconic spots like Strawberry Fields and Bethesda Terrace.

**Empire State Building:** A trip to New York City is incomplete without a visit to the Empire State Building. Ascend to the observation deck on the 86th or 102nd floor for breathtaking panoramic views of the city's skyline.

**Brooklyn Bridge:** An engineering marvel, the Brooklyn Bridge spans the East River and connects Manhattan and Brooklyn. Walk, bike, or simply admire the stunning views of the skyline and the bridge's architectural beauty.

**The Metropolitan Museum of Art:** Known as the Met, this world-renowned museum houses an extensive collection of art spanning thousands of years. Explore its galleries filled with ancient artifacts, European paintings, and contemporary art.

**9/11 Memorial and Museum:** Pay tribute to the victims of the September 11, 2001, terrorist attacks at the 9/11 Memorial, which features two reflecting pools set within the footprints of the Twin Towers. The adjacent museum provides a poignant and informative experience.

**High Line:** Built on a historic elevated freight rail line, the High Line is a unique urban park that stretches along Manhattan's west side. Walk along the landscaped pathways, enjoy art installations, and savor city views.

**Rockefeller Center:** This iconic complex in Midtown Manhattan offers shopping, dining, and entertainment options. Visit the Top of the Rock observation deck for panoramic views, and in winter, don't miss the famous ice skating rink and Christmas tree.

**Broadway:** New York City's Broadway theater district is renowned for its world-class performances. Catch a show at one of the historic theaters and experience the magic of live theater.

These are just a few of the many attractions and landmarks that make New York City a vibrant and captivating destination. Remember to check for any COVID-19 guidelines and restrictions before planning your visit.

## STATUE OF LIBERTY AND ELLIS ISLAND

The Statue of Liberty and Ellis Island are two iconic landmarks located in New York City that hold significant historical and cultural importance. They both played pivotal roles in shaping the history of the United States and continue to serve as symbols of freedom, hope, and opportunity.

The Statue of Liberty, also known as "Lady Liberty," stands tall on Liberty Island in the New York Harbor. Designed by Frédéric Auguste Bartholdi, a French sculptor, and Gustave Eiffel, the renowned engineer behind the Eiffel Tower, the statue represents Libertas, the Roman goddess of freedom. Standing at a height of 305 feet (93 meters), the statue holds a torch in her right hand, symbolizing enlightenment, while her left hand carries a tablet inscribed with the date of the American Declaration of Independence.

The Statue of Liberty served as a welcoming sight for millions of immigrants who arrived in the United States seeking a new life. The statue's significance grew as it became a symbol of hope and freedom for those fleeing persecution, poverty, and war. Its iconic image has been widely featured in various forms of media, making it one of the most recognizable landmarks in the world.

Ellis Island, located in the Upper New York Bay, served as the primary immigration station of the United States from 1892 to 1954. It was the gateway for over 12 million immigrants who passed through its doors in search of the American Dream. Ellis Island was a vital point of entry, where immigrants underwent medical examinations, interviews, and legal inspections to gain entry into the country. For many, it was their first glimpse of America and the beginning of a new chapter in their lives.

Today, Ellis Island is a museum and national historic site, preserving the stories and experiences of those who passed through its halls. Visitors can explore the Ellis Island National Museum of Immigration, which provides an immersive and educational experience, showcasing the personal narratives, photographs, and artifacts of the immigrants who embarked on their American journey through Ellis Island.

The Statue of Liberty and Ellis Island together form a powerful historical and cultural experience. Visitors can take a ferry from Battery Park in Manhattan to Liberty Island and enjoy stunning views of the New York City skyline along the way. The Statue of Liberty itself offers a chance to climb to the observation deck inside the crown or explore the museum in the pedestal. From there, visitors can continue their journey to Ellis Island to delve deeper into the immigrant experience and gain a better understanding of the diverse fabric of American society.

The Statue of Liberty and Ellis Island represent the core values of the United States, including freedom, diversity, and the pursuit of a better life. As symbols of hope and opportunity, they continue to inspire people from all over the world and serve as reminders of the rich immigrant heritage that has shaped America into what it is today.

## TIMES SQUARE AND BROADWAY

Times Square and Broadway are two iconic locations in New York City, known for their vibrant atmosphere and cultural significance.

Times Square is a major commercial intersection in Midtown Manhattan, where Broadway and Seventh Avenue intersect. It is famous for its bright neon billboards, digital screens, and bustling crowds. Times Square is often referred to as "The Crossroads of the World" and is a popular tourist destination. It is particularly famous for its New Year's Eve celebrations, during which a large ball drop takes place at midnight.

Broadway, on the other hand, is a renowned theater district located in the heart of Manhattan. It is home to numerous theaters that showcase a wide range of theatrical performances, including musicals, plays, and other live shows. Broadway is often considered the pinnacle of commercial theater in the United States and attracts theater enthusiasts from around the world.

Many famous shows have premiered and continue to run on Broadway, including long-running hits like "The Phantom of the Opera," "Chicago," "Wicked," and "Hamilton." Broadway shows are known for their high production values, talented performers, and captivating storytelling.

While Times Square and Broadway are interconnected, it's important to note that Times Square refers to the physical location, whereas Broadway specifically pertains to the theater district and the performances that take place there. However, many Broadway theaters are located in or near Times Square, making it a hub of entertainment and excitement. Visitors to Times Square often find themselves immersed in the vibrant energy of Broadway, with theaters, ticket booths, and marquee signs lining the streets.

Both Times Square and Broadway offer unique experiences for locals and tourists alike, with Times Square serving as a bustling hub of activity and Broadway providing world-class theatrical productions.

## CENTRAL PARK

Central Park is a famous and iconic public park located in the heart of Manhattan, New York

City. Spanning 843 acres (341 hectares), it is one of the largest urban parks in the United States and attracts millions of visitors each year. Central Park offers a diverse range of attractions and recreational activities for both residents and tourists to enjoy.

Here are some key features and attractions you can find in Central Park:

**Great Lawn:** This expansive open space is perfect for picnics, sunbathing, and various recreational activities. It also hosts concerts and events.

**Bethesda Terrace and Fountain:** Located at the center of the park, Bethesda Terrace is a beautiful architectural landmark. The fountain is a popular meeting spot and a great place to people-watch.

**Central Park Zoo:** Situated near the southeast corner of the park, the Central Park Zoo is home to a variety of animals, including penguins, sea lions, snow leopards, and more.

**The Mall and Literary Walk:** This scenic promenade is lined with majestic American elm trees and statues of renowned literary figures like William Shakespeare and Robert Burns.

**Belvedere Castle:** Overlooking the park, Belvedere Castle offers panoramic views of Central Park and the Manhattan skyline. It also serves as a visitor center and has exhibits about the park's natural history.

**The Loeb Boathouse:** Located on the edge of the Lake, the Loeb Boathouse offers boat rentals and dining options. It's a great spot for a relaxing boat ride or a meal overlooking the water.

**Conservatory Garden:** Found in the northeastern section of the park, the Conservatory Garden is a serene space with meticulously landscaped gardens, fountains, and manicured lawns.

**Strawberry Fields:** This tranquil section of the park is a memorial dedicated to John Lennon, the famous musician and member of the Beatles. It features the "Imagine" mosaic and is a place for reflection and tribute.

**Wollman Rink:** During the winter months, Wollman Rink transforms into a popular ice-skating destination. Visitors can rent skates and enjoy skating in a picturesque setting.

**Outdoor Activities:** Central Park provides ample opportunities for outdoor activities such as jogging, cycling, horseback riding, and playing various sports like baseball, soccer, and volleyball.

Central Park is a vibrant oasis in the middle of the bustling city, offering a wide array of recreational, cultural, and natural experiences for all to enjoy.

## EMPIRE STATE BUILDING

The Empire State Building stands as an iconic symbol of New York City, proudly dominating the skyline and captivating the imagination of millions of visitors each year. This colossal architectural masterpiece, located in Midtown Manhattan, has become synonymous with the city's grandeur, resilience, and ambition.

Rising to a height of 1,454 feet (443.2 meters) at its antenna tip, the Empire State Building held the title of the world's tallest building for nearly four decades after its completion in 1931. Its design, a blend of Art Deco and modernist influences, reflects the prevailing aesthetic of its era. The building's distinctive setbacks and spire make it instantly recognizable, and its limestone façade exudes elegance and timelessness.

Beyond its awe-inspiring exterior, the Empire
State Building offers a wealth of experiences to
its visitors. The observatories on the 86th and
102nd floors provide breathtaking panoramic
views of the city, where visitors can witness the
bustling streets, Central Park's lush greenery, and
the vastness of the Hudson River. The
observatories have been enhanced with
cutting-edge technology, including
high-definition cameras and interactive displays,
making the visit both educational and
immersive.

Throughout its history, the Empire State
Building has been a witness to countless
significant moments. From its role as a beacon
of hope during the Great Depression to its
commemoration of national milestones and
celebrations, the building has etched itself into

the collective memory of Americans. It has been featured in numerous films, further cementing its status as an enduring cultural icon.

In recent years, it has undergone a significant transformation to become one of the most energy-efficient buildings in the world. With the installation of LED lighting systems, modernized HVAC systems, and other innovative technologies, the building has significantly reduced its carbon footprint and set an example for environmental stewardship.

In conclusion, the Empire State Building is not just an architectural marvel but a symbol of human achievement and aspiration. Its towering presence, stunning views, and rich history make it an essential destination for anyone visiting the vibrant city of New York. Whether day or night, the Empire State Building never fails to inspire awe and captivate the hearts of all who behold it.

## THE METROPOLITAN MUSEUM OF ART

The Metropolitan Museum of Art, commonly known as The Met, is one of the most prominent and largest art museums in the world. Located in New York City, it is situated on the eastern edge of Central Park, along Fifth Avenue. The museum was founded in 1870 and has since become a cultural landmark, housing an extensive collection spanning over 5,000 years of art history.

The Met's collection consists of over two million works of art, covering various disciplines and cultures from around the globe. It includes pieces from ancient Egypt, classical antiquity, European paintings and sculptures, Islamic art, Asian art, African art, American art, and much more. The museum's diverse collection allows visitors to explore a wide range of artistic styles, periods, and mediums.

The museum's main building, known as the "Metropolitan Museum of Art," features grand galleries and exhibition spaces that showcase artworks from different civilizations and time periods. Additionally, The Met Breuer, a separate building located on Madison Avenue, focuses on modern and contemporary art. The Met Cloisters, situated in Fort Tryon Park in Upper Manhattan, is dedicated to medieval European art and architecture.

In addition to its permanent collection, The Met hosts various temporary exhibitions throughout the year, highlighting specific artists, periods, or themes. These exhibitions often attract a large number of visitors and provide a deeper exploration of specific areas of art.

Beyond its artistic treasures, The Met offers educational programs, lectures, workshops, and guided tours for visitors of all ages. The museum's mission is to inspire and engage audiences, fostering a deeper appreciation and understanding of art and culture.

Overall, The Metropolitan Museum of Art is a world-renowned institution that offers a comprehensive and enriching experience for art enthusiasts, scholars, students, and visitors from all walks of life.

# CHAPTER 7

# EXPLORING NEW YORK'S CULTURAL SCENE

Exploring New York City's cultural scene can be an incredibly enriching experience. The city is renowned for its diverse range of cultural offerings, including art, music, theater, dance, museums, and more. Here are some key attractions and activities to consider when exploring New York's vibrant cultural scene:

**Museums:** New York City boasts world-class museums, such as the Metropolitan Museum of Art (MET), Museum of Modern Art (MoMA), Solomon R. Guggenheim Museum, and American Museum of Natural History. Each museum offers a unique collection of art, history, and science exhibits.

**Broadway Shows:** Catching a Broadway show is a must-do in New York City. From classic musicals to contemporary plays, there is a wide variety of performances to choose from. You can check out shows at iconic theaters like the

Richard Rodgers Theatre, Gershwin Theatre, or the Majestic Theatre.

**Music Venues:** New York City is a hub for live music, with venues catering to various genres. You can visit renowned places like Carnegie Hall, Lincoln Center, or Radio City Music Hall for classical and orchestral performances. For smaller, intimate concerts, check out venues like the Bowery Ballroom or the Blue Note Jazz Club.

**Art Galleries:** Chelsea, in Manhattan, is known for its concentration of art galleries. Explore the neighborhood's many galleries and discover contemporary art by both established and emerging artists. The Lower East Side and Williamsburg in Brooklyn also have vibrant art scenes worth exploring.

**Street Art:** New York City's streets are filled with vibrant street art, particularly in neighborhoods like Bushwick, Williamsburg, and the Lower East Side. Take a walk and explore the colorful murals and graffiti art adorning the city walls.

**Cultural Festivals:** Keep an eye out for cultural festivals happening throughout the year. Events like the Tribeca Film Festival, New York Film Festival, New York Fashion Week, and the Celebrate Brooklyn! Performing Arts Festival offer a chance to engage with various art forms and experience the city's cultural diversity.

**Historical Landmarks:** New York City is rich in historical landmarks that provide insights into its cultural heritage. Visit iconic sites like the

Statue of Liberty, Ellis Island, Central Park, Times Square, and the High Line to immerse yourself in the city's history and culture.

**Food and Cuisine:** New York City's culinary scene reflects its multicultural fabric. Explore diverse neighborhoods like Chinatown, Little Italy, Koreatown, or Jackson Heights to indulge in a variety of international cuisines. Additionally, food markets like Chelsea Market and Smorgasburg offer a wide range of food vendors to satisfy your taste buds.

Remember to check the schedules and availability of specific events, exhibitions, or performances beforehand, as they may vary. New York City is constantly evolving, so there's always something new and exciting to discover in its thriving cultural scene. Enjoy your exploration.


## MUSEUMS AND ART GALLERIES


New York City is renowned for its vibrant arts and culture scene, with numerous museums and art galleries to explore. Here are some of the prominent museums and art galleries in New York City:


**The Metropolitan Museum of Art:** Known as "The Met," this world-famous museum features an extensive collection of art spanning 5,000 years from various cultures and civilizations.

**Museum of Modern Art (MoMA):** MoMA is dedicated to contemporary and modern art, showcasing an impressive collection of paintings, sculptures, photographs, films, and design objects.

**Solomon R. Guggenheim Museum:** Designed by Frank Lloyd Wright, the Guggenheim is a masterpiece itself. It focuses on modern and contemporary art and hosts exhibitions of renowned artists.

**Whitney Museum of American Art:** Dedicated to American art, the Whitney Museum presents a vast collection of contemporary and 20th-century works, including paintings, sculptures, films, and performances.

**The Frick Collection:** Housed in the former residence of Henry Clay Frick, this museum features an exceptional collection of European paintings, sculptures, and decorative arts.

**American Museum of Natural History:** While primarily a natural history museum, it also houses an impressive collection of cultural artifacts, including Native American art and artifacts.

**New Museum:** This contemporary art museum focuses on emerging artists and innovative art forms, showcasing cutting-edge exhibitions and installations.

**The Museum of the City of New York:** Dedicated to the history and culture of New York City, this museum offers a range of exhibitions, photographs, and artifacts portraying the city's rich heritage.

**International Center of Photography:** Devoted to photography and visual culture, this museum exhibits a diverse range of photographs, including historic and contemporary works.

**The Morgan Library & Museum:** Housed in a grand building, this museum showcases a remarkable collection of rare books, manuscripts, drawings, and prints, including works by renowned artists like Rembrandt and Picasso.

These are just a few examples of the many museums and art galleries in New York City. The city's cultural landscape is constantly evolving, and there are always new and exciting exhibitions and installations to discover.

## THEATERS AND PERFORMING ARTS

New York City is renowned for its vibrant theater and performing arts scene. Here are some notable theaters and performing arts venues in the city:

**Broadway:** Broadway is synonymous with theater in New York City. It is home to some of the world's most famous theaters, featuring a wide range of musicals, plays, and other live performances. The district stretches along Broadway in Manhattan, particularly in the Times Square area.

**Lincoln Center for the Performing Arts:** Located on the Upper West Side of Manhattan, Lincoln Center is a cultural complex that houses multiple prestigious performing arts organizations. It includes the Metropolitan Opera, New York City Ballet, New York Philharmonic, and numerous theaters hosting a variety of performances.

**Carnegie Hall:** Situated in Midtown Manhattan, Carnegie Hall is a historic concert venue known for its exceptional acoustics. It hosts a diverse range of musical performances, including classical, jazz, world music, and contemporary concerts.

**Radio City Music Hall:** Located in Rockefeller Center, Radio City Music Hall is an iconic venue famous for its Art Deco architecture and the Rockettes. It hosts concerts, stage shows, and special events.

**Off-Broadway:** Apart from the grand theaters of Broadway, New York City also has a thriving Off-Broadway scene. These smaller, more intimate venues showcase a variety of productions, including experimental plays, musicals, and avant-garde performances.

**Public Theater:** The Public Theater, situated in the East Village, is a renowned Off-Broadway theater company. It stages a wide range of productions, including Shakespearean plays, contemporary dramas, and musicals.

**Brooklyn Academy of Music (BAM):** Located in Brooklyn, BAM is a multidisciplinary arts complex that hosts theater, dance, music, and film events. It presents a mix of avant-garde performances, world premieres, and international productions.

**The Metropolitan Opera:** As part of Lincoln Center, the Metropolitan Opera is one of the world's leading opera companies. It stages a diverse repertoire of classic and contemporary operas, attracting renowned singers and conductors from around the globe.

**Joyce Theater:** The Joyce Theater, situated in Chelsea, is a prominent venue for contemporary dance performances. It showcases both established and emerging dance companies, offering a diverse array of styles and genres.

**The Apollo Theater:** Located in Harlem, the Apollo Theater is an iconic venue renowned for showcasing African-American talent. It has a rich history of hosting jazz, R&B, soul, and comedy performances, as well as the famous Amateur Night.

These are just a few examples of the many theaters and performing arts venues in New York City. The city's dynamic arts scene offers something for everyone, with a vast array of performances spanning various genres and styles.

## MUSIC VENUES AND CONCERTS

New York City is renowned for its vibrant music scene, featuring a wide range of music venues and concerts. Here are some notable venues where you can enjoy live music in New York City:

**Madison Square Garden:** Located in Midtown Manhattan, Madison Square Garden is one of the most iconic and prestigious venues in the city. It hosts major concerts by internationally acclaimed artists and has a seating capacity of over 20,000.

**Barclays Center:** Situated in Brooklyn, Barclays Center is a multi-purpose indoor arena that hosts various concerts, including performances by renowned musicians and bands. It is the home arena for the Brooklyn Nets basketball team.

**Radio City Music Hall:** Located in Midtown Manhattan, Radio City Music Hall is a historic venue known for its stunning Art Deco architecture. It hosts a variety of concerts, including large-scale productions, special events, and the famous Christmas Spectacular featuring the Rockettes.

**Beacon Theatre:** Situated on the Upper West Side of Manhattan, the Beacon Theatre is an elegant venue that presents a diverse range of concerts. Known for its excellent acoustics, it attracts both popular musicians and emerging artists.

**Bowery Ballroom:** Located in the Lower East Side of Manhattan, the Bowery Ballroom is a renowned indie music venue. It has a capacity of approximately 550 people and hosts performances by both established and emerging artists.

**Terminal 5:** Situated in Hell's Kitchen, Terminal 5 is a multi-level music venue known for its energetic atmosphere. It can accommodate around 3,000 people and hosts a variety of concerts, including rock, electronic, and alternative music.

**Webster Hall:** Located in the East Village of Manhattan, Webster Hall is one of the city's oldest and most iconic music venues. It features multiple performance spaces and hosts concerts across various genres, including rock, EDM, and hip-hop.

**Irving Plaza:** Situated near Union Square in Manhattan, Irving Plaza is a historic venue that has hosted countless concerts since the 1970s. It has a capacity of approximately 1,000 people and showcases a diverse range of musical acts.

**Carnegie Hall:** Located in Midtown Manhattan, Carnegie Hall is renowned for its exceptional acoustics and prestigious classical music performances. It also hosts concerts across other genres and is considered a cultural landmark.

**The Apollo Theater**: Situated in Harlem, the Apollo Theater is a historic venue with a rich history of showcasing African American talent. It hosts a mix of concerts, including R&B, soul, jazz, and comedy shows.

These are just a few examples of the many music venues and concert halls in New York City. The city offers an array of options to suit different musical tastes, ranging from large arenas to intimate clubs, ensuring there's something for everyone.

## CULTURAL FESTIVALS AND EVENTS

New York City is renowned for its vibrant cultural scene, and there are numerous festivals and events that take place throughout the year. Here are some of the notable cultural festivals and events in New York City:

**Macy's Thanksgiving Day Parade:** Held annually on Thanksgiving Day, this iconic parade features giant balloons, floats, marching bands, and performances. It starts from Central Park West and ends at Macy's Herald Square.

**New York Fashion Week:** This major event takes place twice a year in February and September. It showcases the latest collections of renowned designers and attracts fashion enthusiasts, industry professionals, and celebrities from around the world.

**Tribeca Film Festival:** Founded by Robert De Niro, Jane Rosenthal, and Craig Hatkoff, the Tribeca Film Festival celebrates independent films, documentaries, and emerging filmmakers. It takes place in April and features screenings, premieres, panel discussions, and special events.

**SummerStage:** Presented by City Parks Foundation, SummerStage offers a series of free outdoor concerts, performances, and cultural events in parks across the five boroughs. It showcases a diverse range of music genres, dance, theater, and spoken word performances.

**NYC Pride March:** Held annually in June during LGBTQ+ Pride Month, the NYC Pride March is one of the largest Pride parades in the world. It celebrates the LGBTQ+ community and promotes equality, diversity, and inclusivity.

**New York International Fringe Festival (FringeNYC):** FringeNYC is the largest multi-arts festival in North America. It features an array of performances, including theater, dance, comedy, and music, across various venues in August.

**Governors Ball Music Festival:** This multi-day music festival takes place on Randall's Island in June. It showcases a diverse lineup of popular and emerging artists from various genres, attracting music fans from around the country.

**Feast of San Gennaro:** Celebrated in September, this Italian-American festival is held in the Little Italy neighborhood of Manhattan. It features religious processions, live music, street vendors, carnival games, and delicious Italian food.

**New York Comedy Festival:** This comedy festival brings together some of the biggest names in stand-up comedy for a week of performances in November. It includes shows at renowned comedy clubs and larger venues across the city.

**Diwali at Times Square:** Diwali, the Hindu festival of lights, is celebrated with great enthusiasm in New York City. Times Square hosts a vibrant celebration with cultural performances, traditional music, dance, and delicious Indian cuisine.

These are just a few examples of the many cultural festivals and events that take place in New York City throughout the year. The city's rich cultural diversity ensures there is always something exciting happening to cater to various interests and communities.

# CHAPTER 8

## DINING AND FOOD EXPERIENCES IN NEW YORK

New York City is known for its vibrant culinary scene, offering a wide array of dining and food experiences to suit every taste and preference. Here are some popular dining and food experiences in New York:

**Food Tours:** Take a food tour to explore the diverse neighborhoods of New York and sample a variety of cuisines. Popular food tours include those in Greenwich Village, Chinatown, and Brooklyn, where you can taste everything from pizza and bagels to dim sum and ethnic delicacies.

**Michelin-Starred Restaurants:** New York City boasts numerous Michelin-starred restaurants, offering exquisite dining experiences. Some renowned establishments include Eleven Madison Park, Le Bernardin, Per Se, and

Jean-Georges. These restaurants showcase the finest culinary techniques and use the freshest ingredients.

**Food Markets:** Visit the city's bustling food markets, such as Chelsea Market and Smorgasburg. These markets feature a wide range of food vendors offering diverse cuisines, from gourmet sandwiches and seafood to artisanal chocolates and pastries.

**Iconic Delis:** Don't miss the chance to try classic New York deli sandwiches at establishments like Katz's Delicatessen and Carnegie Deli. These iconic spots serve up piled-high pastrami, corned beef, and other Jewish deli favorites.

**Ethnic Cuisine:** New York City is a melting pot of cultures, resulting in a fantastic selection of authentic ethnic cuisines. Explore the neighborhoods of Little Italy, Chinatown, Koreatown, and Jackson Heights to savor Italian, Chinese, Korean, and Indian cuisines, respectively.

**Food Festivals:** Throughout the year, New York City hosts various food festivals celebrating different culinary traditions. The Taste of Tribeca, New York City Wine & Food Festival, and the Vendy Awards are just a few examples of events where you can sample a wide range of dishes from local restaurants and food trucks.

**Rooftop Dining:** Enjoy stunning views of the city's skyline while indulging in delicious food at rooftop restaurants and bars. Places like The Rooftop at The Standard, 230 Fifth Rooftop Bar, and The Press Lounge offer a memorable dining experience with breathtaking vistas.

**Food Trucks:** New York City is famous for its diverse and delicious food truck scene. From gourmet burgers and tacos to lobster rolls and falafel, food trucks provide a quick and tasty dining experience on the go. Explore popular food truck areas like Midtown and Financial District.

**Dessert Destinations:** Satisfy your sweet tooth at iconic dessert destinations like Serendipity 3, Magnolia Bakery, and Levain Bakery. Indulge in delectable frozen hot chocolate, mouthwatering cupcakes, and irresistible cookies.

**Speakeasies and Cocktail Bars:** New York City is renowned for its speakeasies and craft cocktail bars. Discover hidden gems like PDT (Please Don't Tell), The Dead Rabbit, and Attaboy, where expert mixologists concoct creative and exceptional cocktails.

Remember to make reservations in advance for popular restaurants and be prepared to wait in line at busy food markets or food trucks. New York City offers an abundance of dining and food experiences that cater to all budgets and tastes, ensuring a memorable culinary adventure.

## DIVERSE CUISINE OPTIONS

New York City is renowned for its diverse culinary scene, offering a wide array of cuisine options from all around the world. Whether you're craving traditional dishes or seeking innovative fusion creations, here are some of the diverse cuisine options you can explore in New York City:

**Italian Cuisine:** Visit Little Italy in Manhattan or Arthur Avenue in the Bronx for authentic Italian flavors. You can enjoy classic pasta dishes, wood-fired pizzas, and delectable seafood.

**Chinese Cuisine:** Explore Chinatown in Manhattan for a range of Chinese regional cuisines. From Cantonese dim sum to Sichuan spicy dishes and hand-pulled noodles, you'll find plenty of options to satisfy your cravings.

**Mexican Cuisine:** Head to neighborhoods like East Harlem and the East Village for delicious Mexican fare. Enjoy tacos, enchiladas, mole, and refreshing beverages like horchata and aguas frescas.

**Indian Cuisine:** Curry Hill, located around Lexington Avenue in Manhattan, is home to numerous Indian restaurants. Indulge in aromatic curries, biryanis, dosas, and a variety of vegetarian and vegan options.

**Middle Eastern Cuisine:** Check out areas like Astoria in Queens and the West Village for Middle Eastern delights. Savor kebabs, falafel, shawarma, and traditional Middle Eastern sweets.

**Japanese Cuisine:** Experience sushi, ramen, and other Japanese specialties in areas like Midtown Manhattan or the East Village. Try authentic izakayas, where you can enjoy small plates and sake.

**Korean Cuisine:** Head to Koreatown in Manhattan for Korean barbecue, bibimbap, kimchi, and spicy stews. You can also find trendy Korean fusion restaurants offering unique culinary combinations.

**Thai Cuisine:** Explore the vibrant Thai restaurants in neighborhoods like Hell's Kitchen and Elmhurst, Queens. Sample flavorful curries, pad Thai, spicy salads, and refreshing Thai iced tea.

**Caribbean Cuisine:** Visit neighborhoods such as Flatbush in Brooklyn or Harlem for Caribbean flavors. Enjoy jerk chicken, oxtail stew, roti, and tropical fruits like mango and papaya.

**Ethiopian Cuisine:** Discover the Ethiopian restaurants in the East Village and Harlem. Savor injera (a sourdough flatbread) paired with aromatic stews and vegetable dishes.

These are just a few examples of the diverse cuisine options available in New York City. The city's culinary landscape is constantly evolving, so there are always new and exciting flavors to explore.

## FOOD MARKETS AND STREET FOOD

New York City is renowned for its diverse and vibrant food scene, which includes a wide range of food markets and street food options. Here are some notable food markets and street food experiences you can explore in NYC:

**Chelsea Market:** Located in the Chelsea neighborhood of Manhattan, Chelsea Market is a food lover's paradise. It houses a variety of gourmet food vendors, artisanal shops, and restaurants. You can find everything from fresh seafood and pastries to international cuisines and specialty ingredients.

**Smorgasburg:** Held on weekends in various locations throughout the city, Smorgasburg is a popular outdoor food market. It features a rotating lineup of food vendors offering a wide array of global street food, including tacos,

179

burgers, dumplings, BBQ, ice cream, and much more. The market offers fantastic views along with delicious eats.

**Queens Night Market:** This vibrant night market in Flushing Meadows-Corona Park, Queens, celebrates the diverse culinary traditions of New York City. You can enjoy affordable international street food from all over the world, including Latin American, Caribbean, African, Middle Eastern, and Asian cuisines. The market is known for its lively atmosphere and unique food offerings.

**Essex Street Market:** Located in the Lower East Side of Manhattan, Essex Street Market is a historic indoor market featuring a wide range of food vendors. From fresh produce and seafood to specialty cheeses, baked goods, and international delicacies, you can find a variety of culinary delights here.

**Halal Guys:** If you're craving delicious halal street food, make sure to try the famous Halal Guys food carts. Originating from a humble food cart in Midtown Manhattan, they are now a popular chain with several locations throughout the city. Their menu primarily consists of gyros, chicken, and rice platters smothered in their famous white and hot sauces.

**Food Trucks:** Throughout the city, you'll find numerous food trucks offering diverse cuisines on the go. From gourmet burgers and tacos to Korean BBQ and falafel, these mobile eateries provide a convenient and delicious way to experience street food in NYC. Locations of food trucks can vary, but popular areas like

Midtown, SoHo, and Union Square often have a high concentration of them.

Remember to explore local neighborhoods as well, as you can often find hidden gems like food stands, small bakeries, and ethnic markets offering unique culinary experiences. New York City is a melting pot of cultures, and its food markets and street food scene reflect this wonderfully diverse culinary landscape.

## FINE DINING AND MICHELIN-STAR RESTAURANTS

Fine dining and Michelin-star restaurants are renowned for their exceptional culinary experiences and are often regarded as the pinnacle of gastronomy. Here's some information about them:

**Fine Dining:** Fine dining refers to a type of upscale dining experience that offers exquisite food, elegant ambiance, impeccable service, and attention to detail. These restaurants aim to provide a luxurious and memorable dining experience to their patrons. Fine dining establishments often feature elaborate tasting menus, carefully curated wine lists, and personalized service.

**Michelin Guide:** The Michelin Guide is a prestigious and influential restaurant rating system established by the French tire company, Michelin. The guide assigns Michelin stars to exceptional restaurants, with three stars being the highest accolade. Michelin stars are awarded based on the quality of the cuisine, creativity, technique, consistency, and overall dining experience. Michelin-starred restaurants are known for their exceptional culinary craftsmanship, innovative cooking techniques, and the use of high-quality ingredients.

**Michelin Star Categories:** The Michelin Guide categorizes restaurants into the following star levels:

**One Star:** A restaurant with one Michelin star is considered to have high-quality cuisine and is worth a visit.

**Two Stars:** A two-star restaurant signifies excellent cuisine and is worth a detour for food lovers.

**Three Stars:** The highest distinction, a three-star rating is awarded to restaurants with exceptional cuisine that is worth a special journey. These establishments offer extraordinary culinary experiences and are often considered world-class.

**Criteria for Michelin Stars:** Michelin inspectors evaluate restaurants anonymously, considering several criteria:

**Quality of Ingredients:** The freshness, quality, and sourcing of ingredients used in the dishes.

**Mastery of Flavor and Cooking Techniques:** The skill and precision in cooking, balancing flavors, and creating innovative dishes.

**Chef's Personality:** The chef's culinary identity, creativity, and ability to express their unique style through their cooking.

**Consistency:** The ability of the restaurant to deliver an exceptional dining experience consistently over time.

**Value for Money:** While not a direct factor, Michelin inspectors consider whether the overall dining experience justifies the price.

**Global Presence:** The Michelin Guide covers various countries and cities worldwide, including France, the United States, the United

Kingdom, Japan, Spain, Italy, Germany, Hong Kong, and more. Each edition of the Michelin Guide focuses on a specific region and provides recommendations for the best restaurants in that area.

**Other Restaurant Accolades:** While Michelin stars are highly regarded, there are other prestigious restaurant awards and rankings, such as The World's 50 Best Restaurants, La Liste, and the James Beard Foundation Awards. These accolades also recognize excellence in the culinary world and contribute to the reputation and visibility of top-tier restaurants.

Visiting a fine dining or Michelin-star restaurant offers a unique opportunity to savor exceptional cuisine, experience impeccable service, and indulge in a memorable dining journey.

# CHAPTER 9

# SHOPPING IN THE BIG APPLE

Shopping in New York City, often referred to as the Big Apple, is a dream come true for many avid shoppers. The city offers a wide range of shopping options, from luxury boutiques and department stores to quirky shops and flea markets. Here are some popular shopping destinations in New York City:

**Fifth Avenue:** Known as one of the most prestigious shopping streets in the world, Fifth Avenue is home to iconic stores like Saks Fifth Avenue, Bergdorf Goodman, and Tiffany & Co. You'll find luxury brands, high-end fashion, and upscale department stores along this famous avenue.

**SoHo:** Located in Lower Manhattan, SoHo is a trendy neighborhood with cobblestone streets and a mix of upscale and boutique stores. It's known for its art galleries, designer boutiques, and unique shopping experiences. You can find famous brands like Chanel and Prada, as well as independent fashion labels.

**Herald Square:** Situated near the iconic Empire State Building, Herald Square is home to Macy's, one of the largest department stores in the world. With multiple floors and a vast selection of merchandise, Macy's offers something for everyone. The surrounding area also has other stores, making it a popular shopping district.

**Chelsea Market:** If you're looking for a unique shopping and dining experience, Chelsea Market is a must-visit. Located in the Meatpacking District, this indoor food hall and shopping center features a variety of gourmet food vendors, specialty shops, and artisanal goods.

**Greenwich Village:** Known for its bohemian charm, Greenwich Village offers a mix of vintage boutiques, independent bookstores, and quirky shops. You can explore Bleecker Street, which is famous for its fashion stores, or wander through the neighborhood's winding streets to discover hidden gems.

**Brooklyn Flea Market:** If you enjoy hunting for vintage treasures and one-of-a-kind items, head to the Brooklyn Flea Market. This popular outdoor market features a wide range of vendors selling antiques, clothing, jewelry, artwork, and more. It's a great place to experience the unique and creative spirit of Brooklyn.

**Madison Avenue:** Another upscale shopping destination, Madison Avenue is home to luxury brands like Gucci, Prada, and Chanel. This street spans several blocks on Manhattan's Upper East Side and offers a refined shopping experience with elegant boutiques and high-end retailers.

Remember to plan your shopping trip in New York City based on the areas you want to explore and the specific stores you're interested in. Keep in mind that the city is vast, and it's helpful to research store hours and plan your route to make the most of your shopping experience.

## LUXURY SHOPPING ON FIFTH AVENUE

Luxury shopping on Fifth Avenue in New York City is an iconic experience that offers a wide range of high-end fashion, jewelry, accessories, and more. Fifth Avenue is known for its luxury flagship stores, designer boutiques, and prestigious department stores, making it a prime destination for luxury shoppers from around the world. Here are some of the top luxury shopping destinations on Fifth Avenue:

**Saks Fifth Avenue:** Located between 49th and 50th Streets, Saks Fifth Avenue is a renowned department store offering a curated selection of luxury brands, including fashion, beauty, accessories, and home goods.

**Bergdorf Goodman:** Situated on the corner of Fifth Avenue and 58th Street, Bergdorf Goodman is a luxury department store known for its designer collections, exquisite window displays, and personalized shopping experience.

**Tiffany & Co.:** A legendary jeweler, Tiffany & Co.'s flagship store on Fifth Avenue, near 57th Street, is a must-visit for those seeking exquisite diamonds, engagement rings, and iconic Tiffany jewelry pieces.

**Louis Vuitton:** Located at the corner of Fifth Avenue and 57th Street, the Louis Vuitton flagship store showcases the brand's luxury fashion, accessories, handbags, and luggage in a stunning setting.

**Gucci:** Positioned on the corner of Fifth Avenue and 56th Street, Gucci's flagship store offers a range of high-fashion clothing, shoes, accessories, and leather goods for both men and women.

**Prada:** Situated on Fifth Avenue between 57th and 58th Streets, Prada's flagship store features their signature collection of ready-to-wear fashion, handbags, shoes, and accessories.

**Versace:** Located on Fifth Avenue between 52nd and 53rd Streets, Versace's flagship store showcases their bold and glamorous fashion designs, including clothing, accessories, and home goods.

**Bulgari:** Positioned on the corner of Fifth Avenue and 57th Street, Bulgari is a luxury Italian jeweler offering exquisite watches, jewelry, and accessories.

**Chanel:** Situated on the corner of Fifth Avenue and 57th Street, Chanel's flagship store presents their iconic fashion, accessories, fragrances, and beauty products.

These are just a few examples of the luxury shopping options you'll find on Fifth Avenue. The area also features many other renowned brands, upscale boutiques, and high-end shopping centers, ensuring a luxurious shopping experience for any discerning shopper.

## BOUTIQUE STORES AND INDEPENDENT DESIGNERS

New York City is known for its vibrant fashion scene, and it's home to numerous boutique stores and independent designers. These establishments offer unique and one-of-a-kind fashion pieces, allowing customers to find items that reflect their individual style. Here are some popular areas in New York City where you can explore boutique stores and discover independent designers:

**SoHo:** SoHo (short for South of Houston Street) is renowned for its artistic and trendy atmosphere. This neighborhood is filled with numerous boutique stores and independent designer shops. You'll find a mix of established brands and emerging designers showcasing their creations in areas like Greene Street, Wooster Street, and Mercer Street.

**Nolita:** Nolita, short for North of Little Italy, is a charming neighborhood that features a range of independent boutiques and designer stores. Elizabeth Street and Mulberry Street are particularly popular for their unique fashion offerings, including clothing, accessories, and jewelry.

**Lower East Side:** The Lower East Side has evolved into a trendy destination with an array of boutique stores and independent designers. Explore the area around Orchard Street, Ludlow Street, and Rivington Street to discover hidden gems and fashion-forward pieces.

**Williamsburg, Brooklyn:** While not in Manhattan, Williamsburg in Brooklyn has become a haven for independent designers and boutique shops. Bedford Avenue is the main

198

thoroughfare, lined with a mix of vintage boutiques, concept stores, and local designer shops.

**West Village: The** West Village exudes a quaint and charming vibe, with numerous boutique stores tucked along its streets. Bleecker Street, in particular, is known for its high-end fashion boutiques and independent designers offering unique clothing, shoes, and accessories.

**Chelsea:** Chelsea is home to a mix of art galleries and boutique stores, making it an excellent area to explore independent designers. Along Ninth Avenue, between 16th and 26th Streets, you'll find a diverse selection of boutiques offering a range of fashion choices.

These are just a few examples of areas in New York City where you can find boutique stores and independent designers. It's worth noting that the fashion landscape in the city is ever-changing, with new stores and designers constantly emerging. Exploring these neighborhoods will give you a taste of the city's fashion diversity and allow you to support local designers.

## VINTAGE AND THRIFT SHOPPING

Vintage and thrift shopping in New York City is a popular and exciting activity for fashion enthusiasts and bargain hunters alike. The city offers a wide range of stores and neighborhoods known for their unique vintage finds and secondhand treasures. Here are some tips and

200

recommendations for vintage and thrift shopping in NYC:

**Neighborhoods:** Explore the following neighborhoods known for their vintage and thrift stores:

**Williamsburg, Brooklyn:** This neighborhood is home to numerous vintage boutiques and thrift shops offering a mix of clothing, accessories, and home decor.

**East Village, Manhattan:** Known for its eclectic and edgy vibe, the East Village has an array of thrift stores and vintage shops, particularly along East 9th Street.

Lower East Side, Manhattan: This neighborhood has a mix of vintage stores, designer consignment shops, and thrift stores with unique finds.

**Greenpoint, Brooklyn:** Located near Williamsburg, Greenpoint has a selection of vintage shops with a focus on curated clothing and accessories.

**Beacon's Closet:** With multiple locations in Brooklyn and Manhattan, Beacon's Closet is a popular destination for thrift shopping. They offer a vast selection of secondhand clothing, shoes, and accessories for men and women.

**L Train Vintage:** Another well-known vintage store with several locations in Brooklyn and Manhattan, L Train Vintage is known for its affordable and trendy clothing options.

**Housing Works Thrift Shops:** Housing Works is a nonprofit organization supporting individuals living with HIV/AIDS. They operate thrift shops throughout the city, offering a variety of clothing, furniture, books, and household items.

**Awoke Vintage:** Located in Williamsburg and Greenpoint, Awoke Vintage specializes in curated vintage clothing, accessories, and jewelry.

**Stella Dallas Living:** Situated in the West Village, Stella Dallas Living is a unique store offering vintage clothing, textiles, and home decor from the 1920s to the 1980s.

**Manhattan Vintage Clothing Show:** If you're looking for a special vintage shopping experience, consider attending the Manhattan Vintage Clothing Show. It is held biannually and features a wide range of vintage vendors selling clothing, accessories, and jewelry.

**Flea Markets:** Keep an eye out for flea markets like the Brooklyn Flea, Artists & Fleas, and the Hell's Kitchen Flea Market. These markets often have vintage clothing and antique vendors mixed in with other unique items.

Remember, when vintage and thrift shopping, it's essential to take your time, check the quality of items, and try things on if possible. It's also a good idea to have a budget in mind and be prepared to negotiate prices at some stores or markets. Enjoy your vintage and thrift shopping adventure in NYC!

# FLEA MARKETS AND POP-UP SHOPS

Flea markets and pop-up shops are vibrant aspects of New York City's retail and cultural scene. They offer unique shopping experiences and opportunities to discover one-of-a-kind items, vintage treasures, local crafts, and artisanal goods. Here are a few notable flea markets and pop-up shops in New York City:

**Brooklyn Flea:** Started in 2008, Brooklyn Flea is one of the city's most popular flea markets. It operates in various locations, including Williamsburg and DUMBO, and showcases a wide range of vendors selling vintage clothing, antiques, handmade crafts, jewelry, furniture, and delicious food.

205

**Artists & Fleas:** With locations in Williamsburg, Chelsea Market, and SoHo, Artists & Fleas features a curated selection of independent designers, artists, and vintage collectors. You can find an array of clothing, accessories, home decor, and unique artworks.

**Chelsea Flea Market:** Located in the Hell's Kitchen neighborhood, the Chelsea Flea Market is renowned for its antique and vintage offerings. Open on weekends, it attracts collectors, interior designers, and those seeking vintage clothing, furniture, jewelry, and rare collectibles.

**Grand Bazaar NYC:** This year-round market takes place on the Upper West Side. It hosts over 100 vendors selling vintage and antique items, handmade crafts, artisanal food, and much more.

Grand Bazaar NYC also supports local charities with its profits.

**The Market NYC:** Situated in the heart of SoHo, The Market NYC is a pop-up shop collective featuring emerging fashion designers, artists, and independent brands. It provides a platform for local creatives to showcase their talent and offers a diverse range of clothing, accessories, art, and home decor.

**Canal Street Market:** Located in Chinatown, Canal Street Market is a vibrant space that combines retail, food, and events. It features a mix of pop-up shops, boutiques, art galleries, and food vendors, offering a unique shopping and dining experience.

It's important to note that the availability and specific locations of flea markets and pop-up shops may vary, so it's recommended to check their websites or social media pages for up-to-date information, operating hours, and any entry requirements.

# CHAPTER 10

## NIGHTLIFE AND ENTERTAINMENT

New York City is renowned for its vibrant nightlife and entertainment scene. There are countless options for evening activities, ranging from world-class theaters and live music venues to trendy bars and nightclubs. Here are some popular choices for nightlife and entertainment in NYC:

**Broadway Shows:** Catching a Broadway show is a must-do when in New York City. The Theater District, located in Midtown Manhattan, offers a wide range of productions, from classic musicals to contemporary plays.

**Live Music:** NYC has a thriving live music scene with venues catering to various genres. You can enjoy jazz at the iconic Blue Note or Village Vanguard, rock concerts at Madison Square Garden or Barclays Center, or intimate performances at the Bowery Ballroom or Mercury Lounge.

**Comedy Clubs:** New York City is famous for its stand-up comedy clubs. Places like the Comedy Cellar, Gotham Comedy Club, and Caroline's on Broadway showcase both emerging talent and established comedians.

**Nightclubs:** NYC is home to some of the world's best nightclubs. Venues like Marquee, 1 OAK, and Lavo attract both locals and tourists with top-notch DJs, impressive dance floors, and stylish atmospheres.

**Rooftop Bars:** Enjoy breathtaking views of the city skyline while sipping cocktails at one of NYC's rooftop bars. Popular options include The Press Lounge, Refinery Rooftop, and 230 Fifth.

**Speakeasies:** Step back in time and experience the allure of hidden speakeasies. These secret bars, such as Please Don't Tell (PDT), Attaboy, and Angel's Share, offer a unique and intimate atmosphere for enjoying crafted cocktails.

**Jazz Clubs:** New York City has a rich jazz history, and you can still find exceptional jazz clubs today. The Village Vanguard, Blue Note, and Birdland Jazz Club are renowned venues that showcase talented jazz musicians.

**Nighttime Cruises:** Take a scenic cruise along the Hudson River or around Manhattan Island. You can enjoy dinner, drinks, and live music while taking in the city's stunning skyline.

**Dance Performances:** NYC is a hub for dance, and you can experience world-class ballet, modern, and contemporary dance performances at Lincoln Center, Joyce Theater, and New York City Center.

**Underground Parties:** NYC's underground party scene offers unique and alternative experiences. Keep an eye out for pop-up events, warehouse parties, and secret gatherings that celebrate music, art, and culture.

It's important to note that the availability of specific venues and events may vary, and it's recommended to check for updates and make reservations in advance. NYC's nightlife is ever-changing, and there are always new and exciting experiences to discover in the city that never sleeps.

## BARS AND ROOFTOP LOUNGES

New York City is known for its vibrant nightlife and has numerous bars and rooftop lounges that offer stunning views of the city skyline. Here are a few popular options:

**230 Fifth Rooftop Bar:** Located on Fifth Avenue, this rooftop bar offers breathtaking views of the Empire State Building and the

Manhattan skyline. It has a large indoor/outdoor space, making it a popular spot year-round.

**The Press Lounge:** Situated atop the Ink48 Hotel in Hell's Kitchen, The Press Lounge provides panoramic views of the Hudson River and Midtown Manhattan. It features a sleek and stylish atmosphere, along with a selection of craft cocktails.

**Le Bain:** Positioned on the rooftop of The Standard Hotel in the Meatpacking District, Le Bain offers a trendy and vibrant atmosphere. It features an indoor bar with a glass ceiling and an outdoor terrace with a plunge pool. The rooftop provides beautiful views of the High Line, the Hudson River, and downtown Manhattan.

**The Roof at Public Hotel:** Located on the Lower East Side, The Roof at Public Hotel provides stunning views of the Manhattan skyline. It has a chic and modern design, with both indoor and outdoor seating areas. The bar offers a wide range of cocktails, and it's a great place to enjoy a sunset.

**The Skylark:** Situated in Midtown Manhattan, The Skylark is known for its stylish ambiance and breathtaking views of Times Square and the Empire State Building. It offers a sophisticated rooftop lounge experience, complete with artisanal cocktails and a variety of small plates.

**Refinery Rooftop:** Positioned in the Garment District, Refinery Rooftop offers a rustic yet elegant rooftop experience. It features comfortable seating, lush greenery, and views of the Empire State Building. The bar serves craft cocktails and a selection of American bites.

These are just a few examples, as there are many more rooftop lounges and bars in New York City. It's always a good idea to check their websites or make reservations in advance, as some places may have specific entry requirements or limited seating.

## NIGHTCLUBS AND DANCE HALLS

New York City is known for its vibrant nightlife scene, and it is home to numerous nightclubs and dance halls. These venues cater to a diverse range of musical genres and styles, ensuring that there is something for everyone. Here are a few

notable nightclubs and dance halls in New York
City:

**Output:** Located in Brooklyn, Output was a
popular nightclub known for its cutting-edge
electronic music and state-of-the-art sound
system. However, it permanently closed its doors
in 2019.

**Marquee:** Situated in Manhattan's Chelsea
neighborhood, Marquee is a high-end nightclub
known for its trendy atmosphere and celebrity
sightings. It features a spacious dance floor, VIP
areas, and top-notch DJs spinning a mix of
electronic, hip-hop, and mainstream music.

**Webster Hall:** Located in the East Village,
Webster Hall is one of the oldest and most iconic
nightclubs in New York City. It offers a variety

of rooms and floors, each with a unique ambiance and music style, ranging from EDM and techno to hip-hop and rock.

**Le Bain:** Situated on the rooftop of The Standard hotel in the Meatpacking District, Le Bain is a popular nightclub and lounge with stunning views of the city skyline. It features a heated pool, a dance floor, and a stylish indoor/outdoor space where guests can enjoy electronic and house music.

**Cielo:** Nestled in Manhattan's Meatpacking District, Cielo is a renowned venue for electronic music lovers. It boasts a top-notch sound system and a cozy, intimate atmosphere, making it a favorite among DJs and enthusiasts of house, techno, and deep house music.

**TAO Downtown:** Known for its grandeur and upscale ambiance, TAO Downtown is a multi-level nightclub and restaurant in Lower Manhattan. It offers a combination of dining, lounging, and dancing, featuring a mix of commercial and hip-hop music.

Please note that the nightclub scene is constantly evolving, and new venues may emerge while existing ones may close or change their offerings. It is always recommended to check the latest information, including opening hours and event schedules, before planning a visit to any specific nightclub or dance hall in New York City.

# COMEDY CLUBS AND LIVE PERFORMANCES

New York City is renowned for its vibrant comedy scene, with numerous comedy clubs and live performance venues spread across the city. Here are some popular comedy clubs where you can catch live performances:

**Comedy Cellar:** Located in Greenwich Village, Comedy Cellar is one of the most famous comedy clubs in New York City. It has a reputation for hosting top-notch comedians, including big names like Dave Chappelle, Louis C.K., and Amy Schumer.

**Gotham Comedy Club:** Situated in Chelsea, Gotham Comedy Club features a diverse lineup of talented comedians. It offers a comfortable atmosphere and has been a launching pad for many successful comedians.

**Carolines on Broadway:** Situated in Times Square, Carolines on Broadway is another iconic comedy club. It hosts both well-known and up-and-coming comedians, and its large venue attracts a lively crowd.

**The Stand:** Located in Union Square, The Stand showcases a mix of established and emerging comedians. With a spacious layout and a full-service restaurant, it offers a great comedy and dining experience.

**Upright Citizens Brigade Theatre:** UCB Theatre, with locations in Chelsea and the East Village, is famous for its improv and sketch comedy shows. Many renowned comedians, such as Amy Poehler and Aziz Ansari, have started their careers here.

**New York Comedy Club:** With two locations in Manhattan, New York Comedy Club provides a platform for talented comedians to showcase their skills. It offers a more intimate setting and a variety of shows throughout the week.

These are just a few examples of the many comedy clubs in New York City. It's always a good idea to check their websites or call ahead to confirm showtimes, ticket availability, and any specific requirements or restrictions, as these details can vary.

Additionally, keep in mind that the comedy scene is dynamic, and new clubs and shows may emerge over time, so it's worth exploring local listings and recommendations for the latest happenings in the city's comedy scene.

## LATE-NIGHT EATERIES AND FOOD TRUCKS

New York City is known for its vibrant food scene, and it offers a wide range of late-night eateries and food trucks that cater to different tastes and cravings. Whether you're looking for a quick bite after a night out or a full meal during the late hours, you'll find plenty of options. Here are some popular late-night eateries and food trucks in New York City:

**Late-Night Eateries:**

**Artichoke Basille's Pizza:** Famous for its delicious slices of artichoke pizza, this pizza joint stays open until the early hours of the morning.

**Veselka:** Located in the East Village, Veselka is a 24-hour Ukrainian diner that serves comfort food like pierogies, borscht, and hearty breakfast dishes.

**Pommes Frites**: This East Village spot is known for its Belgian-style fries served with a variety of dipping sauces. It stays open late and is perfect for satisfying your late-night cravings.

**Blue Ribbon Brasserie:** Located in SoHo, Blue Ribbon Brasserie is open until 4 a.m. and offers a diverse menu featuring dishes like fried chicken, oysters, and steak.

**The Meatball Shop:** With multiple locations throughout the city, The Meatball Shop serves up customizable meatball dishes with various sauces and sides until late.

**Food Trucks:**

**Wafels & Dinges:** This popular food truck offers Belgian waffles with a variety of sweet and savory toppings, such as Nutella, strawberries, bacon, and more. You can usually find it in high-traffic areas like Central Park or Union Square.

**Calexico Cart:** Known for its Mexican-inspired cuisine, Calexico Cart serves up delicious tacos, burritos, and quesadillas. The truck can often be found in SoHo and Midtown.

**Korilla BBQ:** Korilla BBQ offers Korean-inspired burritos, tacos, and rice bowls with options like bulgogi beef, spicy pork, and tofu. The truck moves around the city, so check their website or social media for the latest locations.

**Halal Guys:** Famous for its halal street food, the Halal Guys food cart is a New York institution. They serve platters and gyros filled with tender chicken or lamb, rice, and a variety of flavorful sauces.

**El Diablo Tacos:** This food truck specializes in delicious Mexican tacos with fillings like grilled steak, slow-cooked pork, and spicy shrimp. You can find it parked in different locations around the city.

Please note that availability and operating hours of these eateries and food trucks may vary, so it's always a good idea to check their websites or social media for the most up-to-date information before visiting.

# CHAPTER 11

## OUTDOOR ACTIVITIES AND PARKS

New York City offers a wide range of outdoor activities and parks for residents and visitors to enjoy. Here are some popular options:

**Central Park:** Located in the heart of Manhattan, Central Park is an iconic green oasis covering 843 acres. It features beautiful landscapes, meadows, lakes, walking paths, sports fields, playgrounds, and even a zoo. You can go for a leisurely stroll, have a picnic, rent a boat on the lake, or enjoy various recreational activities.

**The High Line:** Built on a historic elevated rail line, the High Line is a unique public park on Manhattan's west side. It offers a scenic walkway with lush vegetation, art installations, and stunning views of the city skyline. It's a great place to relax, take a stroll, and enjoy the urban greenery.

**Brooklyn Bridge Park:** Situated along the Brooklyn waterfront, this park offers fantastic views of the Manhattan skyline. It has green lawns, waterfront promenades, sports fields, playgrounds, and a beautiful carousel. You can also rent bikes or kayaks to explore the park and its surroundings.

**Prospect Park:** Located in Brooklyn, Prospect Park is a large and diverse park designed by the same architects as Central Park. It boasts wooded areas, meadows, a lake, hiking trails, a zoo, and the Prospect Park Bandshell, which hosts concerts and performances during the summer months.

**Governors Island:** Accessible by ferry from Manhattan or Brooklyn, Governors Island is a car-free oasis in the middle of New York Harbor. It offers sprawling lawns, hammocks, bike rentals, art installations, and stunning views of the Statue of Liberty and Lower Manhattan.

**Hudson River Park:** Stretching along the Hudson River on Manhattan's west side, this park offers a variety of recreational activities such as biking, jogging, rollerblading, and fishing. It has sports fields, playgrounds, gardens, and piers with seating areas to relax and enjoy the waterfront.

**Roosevelt Island:** Situated between Manhattan and Queens, Roosevelt Island is a narrow strip of land with parks and promenades along the East River. You can enjoy beautiful views of the city, visit the FDR Four Freedoms Park, or take a ride on the Roosevelt Island Tramway.

**Bronx Zoo and Botanical Garden:** While not traditional parks, these attractions in the Bronx offer vast green spaces to explore. The Bronx Zoo is one of the largest zoos in the United States, while the New York Botanical Garden features stunning gardens, walking trails, and conservatories.

These are just a few examples, but New York City has many other smaller parks, community gardens, and outdoor spaces to discover throughout its five boroughs.

## BOATING AND KAYAKING

Boating and kayaking in New York City can be a fantastic way to enjoy the waterways and experience the city from a different perspective. While New York City is known for its iconic skyline and bustling streets, it also offers various opportunities for boating and kayaking enthusiasts. In particular, remember the following:

**Waterways:** The Hudson River, the East River, and the Atlantic Ocean are just a few of the waterways that surround New York City. Each of these waterways presents unique boating and kayaking opportunities.

**Boating:** There are multiple options for boating in New York City. You can rent motorized boats, sailboats, or yachts from various marinas and boat rental companies. Some popular boating destinations include the Hudson River Park's Pier 25 and Chelsea Piers, where you can find a range of vessels available for rent.

**Kayaking:** Kayaking is a popular activity in New York City, especially in the summer months. The New York City Department of Parks and Recreation operates free public kayaking programs at various locations, such as the Downtown Boathouse on the Hudson River and the Long Island City Community Boathouse on the East River. These programs offer kayaks, paddles, and life jackets for free or at a nominal cost.

**Tours and Classes:** If you're looking for a guided experience or want to improve your skills, many companies offer boating and kayaking tours and classes in New York City. These guided tours provide insights into the city's landmarks and history while enjoying the water. You can find options for sightseeing tours, sunset cruises, and even fishing charters.

**Safety and Regulations:** It's essential to follow safety guidelines and be aware of the regulations when boating or kayaking in New York City. Make sure to wear a life jacket, be mindful of other vessels and pedestrians, and familiarize yourself with the specific rules and regulations governing the waterways.

**Weather and Seasonality:** Boating and kayaking activities in New York City are highly seasonal and depend on weather conditions. The warmer months, typically from late spring to early fall, offer the best opportunities for enjoying water activities.

Remember to check with local authorities or relevant organizations for up-to-date information on boating and kayaking options, safety guidelines, and any specific permits or licenses required. Enjoy your boating and kayaking adventures in the vibrant city of New York!

## HIKING AND NATURE TRAILS

While New York City is primarily known for its bustling streets and iconic landmarks, there are several hiking and nature trails within and around the city where you can escape the urban environment and immerse yourself in nature. Here are a few options:

**Central Park:** Located in the heart of Manhattan, Central Park offers various walking trails and paths that wind through wooded areas, meadows, and around lakes. You can explore spots like the Ramble, a dense forested area, or walk along the Jacqueline Kennedy Onassis Reservoir for a peaceful experience.

**Inwood Hill Park:** Situated at the northern tip of Manhattan, Inwood Hill Park is a beautiful green space with hiking trails that lead through forests and along the Hudson River. The park is known for its natural beauty, including old-growth trees, salt marshes, and the famous "Indian Caves."

**Van Cortlandt Park:** Located in the Bronx, Van Cortlandt Park offers over 1,100 acres of diverse terrain. You can explore woodland trails, open fields, and even hike up Vault Hill, which provides panoramic views of the park. The John Kieran Nature Trail is a popular choice for birdwatching and observing wildlife.

**Staten Island Greenbelt:** On Staten Island, you can find the Staten Island Greenbelt, a network of trails spanning over 2,800 acres of protected land. The trails wind through forests, wetlands, and meadows, providing a peaceful escape from the city. The Greenbelt Nature Center serves as a great starting point for your hike.

**Jamaica Bay Wildlife Refuge:** Located in Queens, the Jamaica Bay Wildlife Refuge is part of the Gateway National Recreation Area. It offers several trails that lead through marshes, ponds, and upland fields. The diverse habitat is home to various bird species, making it a popular spot for birdwatching.

**Palisades Interstate Park:** Just across the Hudson River, you'll find the Palisades Interstate Park, which stretches along the New Jersey side of the river. The park offers stunning views of the cliffs and the river, with numerous hiking trails that wind through forests and overlooks.

These are just a few examples of the hiking and nature trails you can explore within or near New York City. Each of these locations provides an opportunity to reconnect with nature and enjoy some tranquility away from the city's hustle and bustle.

## SPORTS AND RECREATION FACILITIES

New York City is home to a wide range of sports and recreation facilities that cater to both residents and visitors. Here are some of the popular sports and recreation facilities in New York City:

**Central Park:** Central Park is one of the most iconic and expansive recreational spaces in New York City. It offers numerous opportunities for outdoor activities, including running, cycling, tennis, baseball, soccer, and horseback riding. The park also has several playgrounds, skating rinks, and a public swimming pool.

**Chelsea Piers:** Located on the Hudson River, Chelsea Piers is a massive sports and recreation complex. It features state-of-the-art facilities for various sports such as basketball, volleyball, soccer, golf, ice skating, and rock climbing. Chelsea Piers also offers fitness centers, a spa, and a bowling alley.

**Flushing Meadows-Corona Park:** This park in Queens hosted the 1964 World's Fair and is now a popular destination for sports and recreation. It has facilities for tennis, soccer, baseball, cricket, and running. Flushing Meadows also includes the USTA Billie Jean King National Tennis Center, where the US Open tennis tournament takes place.

**Rockaway Beach and Boardwalk:** Located in Queens, Rockaway Beach is the largest urban beach in the United States. It provides opportunities for swimming, surfing, volleyball, and sunbathing. The adjacent boardwalk is perfect for walking, jogging, and cycling.

**The Armory Track & Field Center:** The Armory is an indoor track and field facility in Washington Heights, Manhattan. It hosts numerous track and field events, including high school and college competitions. The Armory also offers public access for running and fitness activities.

**Asphalt Green:** Asphalt Green is a sports and fitness center with two locations in Manhattan's Upper East Side and Battery Park City. It provides facilities for swimming, basketball, soccer, gymnastics, and fitness classes. Asphalt Green also offers a variety of youth and adult sports programs.

**Chelsea Waterside Park:** Situated along the Hudson River in Chelsea, this park offers recreational amenities such as basketball and volleyball courts, a soccer field, a playground, and a water park during the summer months.

**Pelham Bay Park:** Pelham Bay Park is the largest park in New York City, located in the Bronx. It encompasses over 2,700 acres and offers facilities for golfing, tennis, horseback riding, baseball, and hiking. The park also has a sandy beach called Orchard Beach.

**Indoor Ice Skating Rinks:** New York City has several indoor ice skating rinks, including the iconic Rockefeller Center Ice Rink, the Chelsea Piers Sky Rink, and the City Ice Pavilion in Queens. These rinks offer public skating sessions, figure skating lessons, and hockey programs.

**Recreational Centers:** The New York City Parks Department operates various recreational centers throughout the city. These centers provide fitness equipment, swimming pools, basketball courts, and organized sports activities for all ages.

These are just a few examples of the sports and recreation facilities available in New York City. The city offers a wide array of options for sports enthusiasts and those looking to engage in recreational activities.

# CHAPTER 12

# PRACTICAL INFORMATION AND SAFETY TIPS

Here are some practical information and safety tips for visiting or living in New York City:

**Transportation:**

**Public transportation:** New York City has an extensive public transportation system, including subways, buses, and commuter trains. The subway is a convenient and efficient way to get around the city.

**Taxis and rideshares:** Taxis and rideshare services like Uber and Lyft are widely available in the city.

**Walking:** New York City is a walkable city, and many attractions are within walking distance of each other.

Safety:

**Stay aware of your surroundings:** Like in any large city, it's important to stay vigilant and aware of your surroundings, especially in crowded areas.

**Secure your belongings:** Keep your personal belongings secure and be cautious of pickpockets, especially in crowded places and on public transportation.

**Use well-lit and busy streets:** Stick to well-lit and populated streets, particularly at night.

**Emergency services:** In case of an emergency, dial 911 for police, fire, or medical assistance. Neighbourhoods:

**Research neighbourhoods:** New York City has many diverse neighbourhoods, each with its own character. Before visiting or moving to a particular neighbourhood, research its safety reputation and familiarize yourself with the local environment.

**Avoid unsafe areas**: While most areas in New York City are safe for tourists and residents, it's advisable to avoid certain high-crime areas, especially at night.

**Scams and street vendors:**

**Be cautious of scams**: Be aware of common scams targeting tourists, such as fake tickets, overcharging, and street games aimed at taking your money. Avoid engaging with aggressive street vendors.

**Purchase from licensed vendors**: If you plan to buy souvenirs or food from street vendors, choose licensed vendors to ensure quality and safety.

**Emergency preparedness:**

**Familiarize yourself with emergency exits:** Whether you're in a hotel, shopping center, or any public place, take note of emergency exits and evacuation plans.

**Have emergency contacts**: Keep a list of important contacts, including your embassy or consulate, local hospitals, and emergency services.

**Stay informed:** Stay updated on local news, weather conditions, and any emergency alerts during your stay.

**COVID-19 precautions:**

**Follow guidelines:** Stay updated on the latest COVID-19 guidelines and regulations set by local authorities and health organizations. This includes wearing masks, practicing social distancing, and following capacity limits in public spaces.

**Get vaccinated:** If eligible, consider getting vaccinated against COVID-19 before your visit.

Check venue policies: Before visiting attractions, restaurants, or events, check their COVID-19 policies and requirements.

Remember, New York City is generally a safe place, but taking basic precautions and being aware of your surroundings can help ensure a smooth and enjoyable experience.

## CURRENCY, TIPPING, AND TAXES

**Currency**:

The currency used in New York City, as well as the rest of the United States, is the United States Dollar (USD). Cash is widely accepted in most places, including restaurants, taxis, and small businesses. However, credit and debit cards are also commonly used, and many establishments, especially larger businesses, accept digital payment methods such as Apple Pay, Google Pay, and contactless cards.

**Tipping:**

Tipping is a customary practice in the United States, including New York City, and is expected for various services. Here are some general guidelines for tipping in common situations:

**Restaurants:** It is customary to tip around 15-20% of the total bill before taxes. Some restaurants may automatically include a service charge for larger groups, so check the bill to avoid overtipping.

**Bartenders:** A tip of $1-2 per drink or 15-20% of the total bill is customary.

**Taxis and Rideshares:** Tipping taxi drivers and rideshare drivers (such as Uber or Lyft) is common. It is customary to tip around 15-20% of the total fare. For smaller amounts, rounding up to the nearest dollar is also acceptable.

**Hotel Services:** For bellhops who assist with luggage, a tip of $1-2 per bag is customary. Housekeeping staff can be tipped $2-5 per day, left in an envelope or with a note indicating that it is for them.

**Other Services:** Tipping is also expected for services like hairdressers, spa treatments, tour guides, and similar services. The typical tip ranges from 15-20% of the total cost.

Remember that tipping is discretionary, and you can adjust the percentage based on the quality of service received.

**Taxes:**

Sales tax is applied to most goods and services in New York City. The current combined sales tax rate in New York City is around 8.875%. However, specific tax rates may vary depending on the type of goods or services being purchased. The sales tax is added to the total price at the time of purchase.

It's important to note that this information is accurate as of my knowledge cutoff in September 2021, and there may have been changes to tax rates or tipping customs since then. It's always a good idea to check the latest information or consult local resources for the most up-to-date details.

## EMERGENCY SERVICES AND MEDICAL FACILITIES

New York City has a well-developed emergency services and medical facilities system to cater to the needs of its residents and visitors. Here's an overview of emergency services and medical facilities available in New York City:

**Emergency Medical Services (EMS):** The New York City Fire Department (FDNY) operates the EMS system in the city. EMS provides pre-hospital emergency medical care and transportation to hospitals. They have a fleet of ambulances strategically located throughout the city, ready to respond to medical emergencies.

**Hospitals:** New York City is home to numerous hospitals, including some world-renowned medical centers. These hospitals offer a wide range of medical services, including emergency departments, specialized care, surgeries, and comprehensive medical treatments. Some prominent hospitals in New York City are NewYork-Presbyterian Hospital, Mount Sinai Hospital, NYU Langone Medical Center, and Bellevue Hospital Center.

**Trauma Centers:** New York City has designated trauma centers equipped to handle severe and life-threatening injuries. These centers provide specialized care for trauma patients, including those involved in accidents, major falls, or incidents requiring critical care. Some of the trauma centers in the city include the Level I Trauma Centers at Bellevue Hospital Center, Jacobi Medical Center, and NewYork-Presbyterian/Weill Cornell Medical Center.

**Urgent Care Centers:** Urgent care centers offer medical care for non-life-threatening conditions that require immediate attention but do not require an emergency room visit. These centers provide services for minor injuries, illnesses, infections, and other urgent medical needs. There are numerous urgent care centers spread across the city, offering extended hours and walk-in appointments.

**Poison Control Center:** The New York City Poison Control Center provides 24/7 emergency assistance and information regarding poisoning incidents. They offer guidance on poison exposures, including household products, medications, chemicals, and other substances. In case of a poisoning emergency, you can contact them at (800) 222-1222.

**Mental Health Services:** New York City has a comprehensive mental health support system to address the needs of its residents. The NYC Well program offers mental health support and resources 24/7. They provide phone counseling, crisis intervention, and referrals to mental health services. Additionally, there are mental health clinics and facilities throughout the city that offer a range of services.

In case of an emergency, dial 911 to contact emergency services. They will dispatch appropriate help, including police, fire, or medical assistance, depending on the situation. It's important to remember that if you are experiencing a life-threatening emergency, the nearest emergency room is the most appropriate place to seek immediate medical attention.

## STAYING SAFE IN NEW YORK

Staying safe in New York, or any city for that matter, is important to ensure a positive experience and avoid potential risks. Here are some tips to help you stay safe while in New York:

**Be aware of your surroundings:** Pay attention to your surroundings at all times, especially in crowded areas or at night. Stay alert and trust your instincts if something feels off.

**Stick to well-lit and populated areas:** Stick to well-populated streets and avoid poorly lit or deserted areas, particularly at night. Walking on well-traveled routes decreases the likelihood of encountering potential dangers.

**Secure your belongings:** Keep your belongings secure to minimize the risk of theft. Use bags with secure closures, and avoid displaying expensive items like jewelry, electronics, or large amounts of cash in public.

**Use reputable transportation:** Stick to licensed taxis, rideshare services, or public transportation options provided by the Metropolitan Transportation Authority (MTA). Avoid using unlicensed or unofficial transportation services.

**Keep important documents safe:** Make photocopies or take pictures of your important documents such as passport, visa, and identification cards. Keep the originals in a secure location, like a hotel safe, and carry the copies with you while exploring the city.

**Stay cautious with strangers:** Be cautious when interacting with strangers, especially if they approach you with unsolicited offers or requests. Use your judgment and avoid sharing personal or financial information with people you don't know.

**Be careful with ATMs and card transactions:** Use ATMs located in well-populated and well-lit areas. Shield your PIN while entering it, and be cautious of anyone standing too close or behaving suspiciously. When making card transactions, keep an eye on your card and ensure it is returned to you promptly.

**Use reputable accommodations:** Choose reputable hotels or accommodations with good reviews and security measures in place. Lock your room when you leave and utilize the hotel safe for valuable items.

**Emergency services:** Familiarize yourself with the emergency contact numbers in New York, such as 911, and know the location of the nearest police stations, hospitals, and fire departments.

**Stay updated on local news and advisories:** Keep yourself informed about the latest news, events, and any safety advisories related to New York City. This will help you stay aware of any potential risks or concerns.

Remember, while these tips can help enhance your safety, there is no guarantee of absolute security. Always use your common sense, trust your instincts, and take necessary precautions to ensure your well-being while exploring New York.

## LOCAL LAWS AND REGULATIONS

Here are some key areas of local laws and regulations in New York City:

**Housing Laws:** New York City has specific laws governing rent stabilization, rent control, and tenant rights. The city has regulations on rent increases, eviction procedures, and building maintenance standards. The New York City Housing Authority (NYCHA) oversees public housing programs.

**Employment Laws:** New York City has its own employment laws, which may go beyond state and federal requirements. These laws cover areas such as minimum wage, paid sick leave, workplace discrimination, sexual harassment, and worker protections.

**Consumer Protection:** The city has consumer protection laws in place to safeguard consumers from deceptive business practices. These laws cover areas such as price gouging, false advertising, and consumer rights.

**Business Regulations:** New York City has specific regulations for starting and operating businesses. These regulations include licensing requirements, zoning laws, health and safety standards, and permits for certain activities.

**Traffic and Transportation:** The New York City Department of Transportation (NYC DOT) regulates traffic and transportation within the city. This includes rules related to parking, street signage, bike lanes, public transportation, and pedestrian safety.

**Environmental Regulations:** The city has various environmental regulations aimed at preserving and protecting the environment. These regulations cover areas such as waste management, air quality, water conservation, and energy efficiency.

**Noise Control:** New York City has noise control regulations to maintain quality of life for residents. These regulations set limits on noise levels from construction sites, businesses, and other sources, especially during nighttime hours.

**Health and Safety Regulations:** The New York City Department of Health and Mental Hygiene (DOHMH) enforces health and safety regulations. These regulations cover areas such as food safety, sanitation, tobacco control, and public health emergencies.

It's important to note that this is not an exhaustive list, and there are many other local laws and regulations in New York City. If you have specific questions or need detailed information on a particular topic, it's recommended to consult official sources such as the New York City government website or seek legal advice.

# CONCLUSION

In conclusion, "New York First-Timer Travel Guide" is an invaluable resource for anyone planning their first visit to the vibrant and diverse city of New York. The book offers a comprehensive and well-organized collection of information, tips, and recommendations that will help first-time travelers make the most of their experience.

One of the book's greatest strengths is its attention to detail. It covers a wide range of topics, including accommodation options, transportation, iconic landmarks, cultural attractions, dining, shopping, and entertainment. The authors provide practical advice on navigating the city's bustling streets, utilizing public transportation, and maximizing one's time and budget.

The guidebook not only highlights the popular tourist destinations such as Times Square, Central Park, and the Statue of Liberty but also delves into lesser-known neighborhoods and hidden gems that offer a more authentic New York experience. It encourages readers to explore beyond the typical tourist attractions and discover the city's unique neighborhoods, each with its own distinct character and charm.

The inclusion of maps, suggested itineraries, and useful contact information further enhances the book's usefulness. Readers can easily plan their days, select attractions based on their interests, and find their way around the city with ease.

Additionally, the book provides insights into the city's rich history, cultural diversity, and artistic heritage, helping visitors understand the context and significance of the places they are exploring. It also offers practical advice on etiquette, safety, and local customs, ensuring that readers feel prepared and confident during their visit.

Overall, "New York First-Timer Travel Guide" is an indispensable companion for anyone embarking on their first journey to the Big Apple. Its comprehensive coverage, practical advice, and insider tips will help travelers make the most of their time in the city, ensuring a memorable and enjoyable experience. Whether it's admiring iconic landmarks, immersing in the city's vibrant culture, or savoring its culinary delights, this guidebook is a valuable resource that will enhance any first-time visitor's trip to New York.

## RECOMMENDED WEBSITE AND APPS

There are numerous websites and apps that can enhance your experience in New York City. Here are some popular recommendations:

**Website:** Time Out New York (www.timeout.com/newyork)
Time Out New York is a comprehensive online guide to events, activities, restaurants, and entertainment in the city. It provides up-to-date information on things to do, places to visit, and where to eat and drink.

**App: Citymapper**

Citymapper is an excellent app for navigating public transportation in New York City. It offers real-time updates on subway and bus routes, as well as alternative transportation options like biking and ride-sharing. The app provides detailed directions and estimated travel times, making it easy to get around the city efficiently.

**Website:** Official New York City Guide (www.nycgo.com)

The Official New York City Guide is a website that offers comprehensive information on attractions, events, dining, shopping, and more. It is an official resource provided by NYC & Company, the city's official tourism organization.

## App: Yelp

Yelp is a popular app for finding restaurants, bars, and other businesses in New York City. It features user reviews, ratings, and photos to help you make informed decisions about where to eat, drink, or visit.

**Website:** The High Line (www.thehighline.org)
If you're interested in exploring the unique elevated park, The High Line, in New York City, their official website provides information about upcoming events, art installations, and park hours. You can learn about the history of The High Line and plan your visit accordingly.

## App: Central Park Official App

For visitors interested in Central Park, the Central Park Official App is a useful resource. It provides maps, walking routes, guided tours, and information.

Printed in Great Britain
by Amazon